Vinegars:
The Miracle Food

Céline Trégan

Vinegars: *The Miracle Food*

More than 175 Recipes and Practicle Tips to Clean, Cook, Garden, Heal, Loose Weight and Pamper

cardinal

Céline Trégan

Vinegar: The Miracle Food

Graphic design and layout: David Savard, Réaktion
Graphic design of English version: Luc Sauvé
Cover photography and photography of recipes: Tango
Food stylist: Véronique Gagnon-Lalanne
Additional photography: Claude Charlebois and Julie Léger
English translation: Lorien Jones
Copy editing: Emily Raine

ISBN: 978-2-920943-78-0

Legal Deposit: 2012
Bibliothèque et Archives du Québec
Library and Archives Canada
ISBN: 978-2-920943-78-0

The publisher acknowledges the financial support of the Government of Canada through the Canada Book Fund (CBF) for its publishing activities and the support of the Government of Quebec through the tax credits for book publishing program (SODEC).

Printed in Canada

Table of Contents

PART 1

Vinegar

Vinegar: A Rich History

The Legend of Cleopatra's Pearls

L egend has it that Cleopatra owned two gigantic pearls, gifts from Oriental kings. While Mark Antony was a guest in her realm, he indulged in day after day of splendid banquets. Cleopatra, who was vain and arrogant, scorned these lavish feasts. One day, Mark Antony asked what could possibly be added to such extravagance that would convince her to join him at the table. Cleopatra said that he must watch her spend ten million sesterces over the course of one meal. Dumbfounded by this request, Mark Antony declared it impossible.

The queen challenged the Roman general, betting him that it could indeed be done, and that she herself would swallow the sesterces. Skeptical, Mark Antony immediately accepted. The next day, she served him the usual sumptuous meal. When the second course was set, servants placed a single vessel filled with vinegar in front of Cleopatra. The queen removed one of the two pearls adorning her ears and dropped it into the liquid. After the pearl dissolved, she drank the mixture down in a single swallow.

Mark Antony had been defeated.

Vinegar in the Ancient World

Numerous texts, many more than 2,000 years old, describe vinegar as an everyday ingredient. In fact, certain Bible passages show that the Hebrews were familiar with its properties, including its ability to dissolve calcium. Honey vinegar, derived from mead, was already commonly used at the time. Legend tells that Helen of Troy, mythical daughter of Tyndareus, King of Sparta, bathed in vinegar for relaxation.

In classical times, vinegar was mainly used for its therapeutic, antiseptic, astringent and refreshing properties. Starting in 400 BCE, the famous Ancient Greek physician Hippocrates, considered the father of Western medicine, prescribed it to his patients as a remedy for insect bites, inflammation, fever, and bleeding. In his agriculture manual, Cato the Elder wrote that olive pickers, in addition to their regular pay, received an "allocation of vinegar." Romans also treated many illnesses with cabbage and vinegar, and one written account recommends that "if you wish to eat and drink in excess, first eat raw cabbage pickled in vinegar."

Vinegar was likely the first antibacterial medicine in history. The Babylonians discovered that vinegar slowed the spread of bacteria that caused food to rot; they also used it as a preservative, condiment, and seasoning. From 2,000 BCE onward, the Chinese used rice vinegar for cleaning and seasoning dishes. India has also been making vinegar from palm sap or sago[1] for several thousand years.

---

1   *The sago palm is a palm tree cultivated in intertropical regions.*

Vinegar: A Refreshing Beverage

The Romans made a bitter wine called posca with watered-down vinegar (prepared from sour wine spoiled by poor preservation), sometimes mellowed by adding egg yolk. Posca was given to slaves, the Roman army, and the lower classes, and was a popular beverage because it was a very effective thirst quencher when mixed with water. When a soldier gave it to a dying torture victim, he was simply offering the victim his or her everyday beverage. It was a gesture of charity to relieve thirst and not intended to inflict more suffering on the condemned prisoner. In fact, Roman soldiers gave Jesus posca during his crucifixion.

During the reign of Claudius, Scribonius Largus assembled his own collection of recipes, *Compositiones*, in which he describes a *dentifricium* composed of barley flour, vinegar, burnt honey, mineral salt, and nard oil[2] that he claimed would brighten teeth to a glimmering white and prevent them from falling out.

During the Roman Empire, a traditional meal usually started with eggs and ended with a serving of fruit. Romans were great aficionados of sweet-and-sour foods, and fruit was also often used in savory dishes along with garum[3] and vinegar. In Palestine, water and vinegar was an everyday drink. The Song of Solomon mentions wine that is "aged, with mingling flavors of herbs and spices and pomegranate juice." Palestinian field workers also drank vinegar and water, and used it as a dip for bread during the hotter months of the year.

---

2   *Nard essential oil comes from Northern India and has been used for thousands of years for its therapeutic properties and as a perfume. It is an aromatic plant from the same family as valerian.*

3   *Fish-based sauce.*

The Greeks used vinegar to purify and refresh water. During meals, they dipped bread in vinegar or used it to season dishes. As a beverage, water with vinegar was considered better for digestion than just water. Plain vinegar was also prized for its therapeutic uses, as it was believed to purify unwholesome air and help treat and prevent plague.

In one ancient text, the historian Livy recounts Hannibal's famous crossing of the Alps in mid-October, 218 BCE. Upon discovering that his intended route through the mountains was impassable, Hannibal ordered his soldiers to cut down the large surrounding trees and build a great bonfire. When a strong wind blew, causing the fire to heat the rocky path, Hannibal observed that he could use vinegar to break the rockfall, allowing his army to pass through.

Cooking with Vinegar: The Medieval Taste for Sweet and Sour

During the Middle Ages, frequent waves of plague continued to strike a population already weakened by war and economic hardship. Physicians of the era recommended a spice-free diet, as the warming nature of spices was thought to promote the spread of illness, and they endorsed the use of vinegar for all purposes: as mouth rinses, nasal drops and masks, and as seasoning for dishes.

The preparation of flavor-enhancing products, such as vinegar- and verjuice-based[4] sauces and mustards, was refined and improved during the Middle Ages. French cuisine in the 14th century favored acidic flavors, and today, around 70% of French recipes use acidic ingredients like wine, vinegar, verjuice, and currants. Many French sauces are extremely acidic, including a classic green sauce[5] made from "bread, parsley, ginger, and verjuice or vinegar." Also popular in medieval cuisine was the medley of sweet and sour flavors using sugar, honey, or fruit left out to "age."

---

4   *Verjuice is the acidic juice made by cold-pressing unripe green grapes. It was commonly flavored with spices,* fines herbes, *lemon juice, green grape juice, or sorrel.*

5   *Green sauce is a basic sauce made from chopped* fines herbes *(shallots, chervil, watercress, tarragon, spinach, parsley, etc.) mixed with mayonnaise. Many versions of this recipe exist.*

Food preservation methods were also vastly improving at that time. Medieval cooks were learning how to conserve in sugar or honey and in salt or vinegar. When sugar began to appear in recipes in the 15th century, these new, sweeter flavors transformed the taste of strong, spicy dishes and acidic, vinegary dishes.

Vinegar "marinades" were developed during the 17th century, when recipes for pickles as well as sardines or tuna conserved in vinegar first appeared. Natural ingredients such as salt, vinegar, and even saltpetre were used to preserve meats and certain vegetables. The advances made in pickling cucumbers and other vegetables in vinegar — a highly valued culinary practice in India — ensured the introduction of cucumbers to the occidental world. Colonizing countries also influenced the cuisine in certain regions of India, particularly in the state of Goa, which was a Portuguese colony until 1961. Meat was shipped by boat from Portugal, tightly sealed in wooden barrels in a mixture of vinegar or white wine, garlic, bay leaves, and paprika, which preserved the meat during the long voyage. In India, the meat was cooked using local spices, and dishes such as pork vindaloo[6] were created.

---

6   *"Vindaloo" comes from "vinha d'alhos," a basic Portuguese marinade made with white wine, garlic, bay leaves, and paprika.*

The Guild of Vinegar and Mustard Makers

The demand for vinegar was so great during the Middle Ages that making vinegar finally became a true profession, and a small industry developed around it. In 1394, French, Italian, and Spanish vinegar and mustard[7] makers joined together to form an exclusive guild. To become members, these culinary artists took an oath, swearing never to reveal the secrets of the trade. The vinegar maker's guild of Orleans controlled the fabrication and trade of vinegar, verjuice and mustard. In 1580, Henry III issued a letters patent declaring the profession of vinegar and mustard makers to be a "sworn profession in the city and its suburbs."

But up until the 17th century, vinegar was just a by-product of wine and beer. Orleans was a major river port city and half of all French vinegar was produced there, even though the city itself didn't have a vineyard. The transportation of barreled wine from Angers and Touraine to Paris via the Loire River was slowed by shipwrecks and variations in river flow, so wines shipped from these regions frequently turned sour during the long, grueling journey due to heat and poor navigation conditions, and were often unpalatable by the time they reached Orleans. This sour wine would be offloaded at Orleans to be made into vinegar. Production gradually shifted to the city of Dijon. There, Jean Naigeon revolutionized the formula for strong mustard by substituting verjuice (the sour juice of unripe grapes) for vinegar, and the world-famous Dijon mustard was born. Made from hulled black mustard seeds blended with white wine vinegar and spices, Dijon mustard is now protected by an *appellation d'origine contrôlée* obtained in 1937.

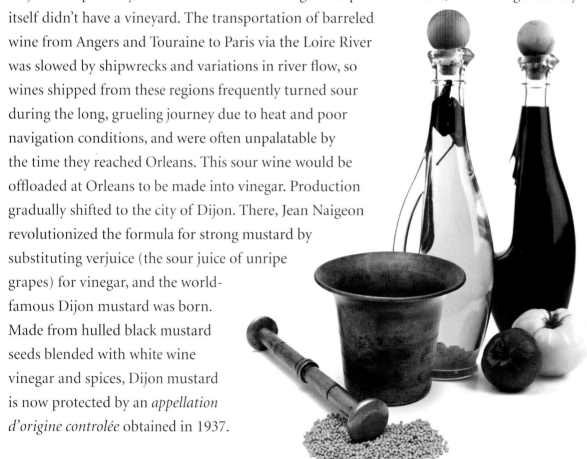

---

7   *Three thousand years ago, the Chinese were the first to blend ground mustard seeds with an acidic juice extracted from grapes to create the condiment we now know as mustard. But it was during the lavish celebrations held by the dukes of Burgundy that the city of Dijon became synonymous with the mustard, making the condiment a symbol of luxury and sophistication.*

The Legend of the Four Thieves

*I*n the year 1720, Marseillais officials were fighting a losing battle against the ravages of plague, which would decimate over a third of the population. According to legend, the city was being plundered by four ruthless thieves who seemed to be immune to the disease, allowing them to enter homes and rob plague victims without becoming infected. When the thieves were finally caught, the judge offered them a more lenient sentence in exchange for the secret that protected them from the deadly disease. Under torture, they finally admitted that they had concocted a special vinegar, which they would drink daily and rub on their bodies, hands, and faces. In exchange for this confession, the thieves were hanged instead of burned alive. Officials distributed the recipe to the townspeople, who from then on tied sponges to their mouths soaked in Four Thieves Vinegar to avoid catching plague.

Four Thieves Vinegar was added to the *Codex* in 1748 because of its dermatological and antiseptic disease-fighting properties and was sold in pharmacies as an external antiseptic until 1937.

Traditional Recipe for Four Thieves Vinegar

- 4 tsp rosemary
- 4 tsp sage
- 4 tsp mint
- 4 tsp rue
- 1 tbsp sweet flag
- 1 tbsp garlic
- 4 tsp lavender
- 4 tsp thyme
- 4 tsp wormwood
- 1 tbsp cinnamon
- 1 tbsp cloves
- 1 tsp camphor

Mix all ingredients with 6 cups of cider vinegar. Leave mixture to steep for 10 days. Strain and store in a cool, dark place..

Another document declares that perfuming the body is important for plague prevention and daily care, and recommends rubbing vinegar onto the face and hands. The acidic, aromatic, and refreshing scent was believed to disinfect and purify the body and mask the odor of decomposition associated with plague.

Antoine-Claude Maille is the credited inventor of "Four Thieves Vinegar," and various accounts declare that Maille created "a mixture with antiseptic properties that, when applied to the body, prevented contagion and saved many lives as a result." It was only during its second generation, however, that the House of Maille truly achieved success, mainly because of its cleansing vinegars. In fact, at the time the House of Maille was producing up to two hundred cleansing and scented vinegars. In 17th century Europe and England, vinegar was mostly used to mask foul odors; townsfolk would hold vinegar-soaked sponges to their noses to block the smell of the open sewers. Women kept sponges dipped in vinegar in small silver boxes, while men carried vinegared sponges in their walking sticks. Even the powerful British Royal Navy used vinegar, both to preserve food during long voyages and to wash ship decks.

What Is Vinegar?

The Biochemistry of Vinegar

In 1730, Dutch chemist Hermann Boerhaave identified the difference between alcohol fermentation (the conversion of sugars into alcohol), acetic fermentation (the conversion of alcohol into vinegar), and putrid fermentation (the putrefaction of wine). German chemist and physician George Ernst Stahl also succeeded in specifying alcohol as the key to the acetic fermentation process. In 1822, Dutch botanist Christiaan Hendrik Persoon discovered *acetobacter*, the microorganism responsible for fermentation. Believing it to be a fungus, he named it *mycoderma aceti* and attributed the production of vinegar to the substance that accumulates on the surface of wine exposed to the open air. In actual fact, this substance is composed of acetic bacteria belonging to the genera *acetobacter* and *gluconobacter*. In 1863, Louis Pasteur finally identified the accurate process of, and ingredients necessary for, vinegar fermentation, and in 1865, his theory of the biochemical nature of vinegar production was established as scientific fact. Thanks to Pasteur's research, the industrial production of vinegar boomed.

From Wine to Vinegar

The word "vinegar" comes from the French *vinaigre,* a combination of the words *vin* (wine) and *aigre* (sour). Vinegar varies in color and contains no protein or fat. It is low in carbohydrates and calories and produced from foods found in nature, including fruit (apples, grapes, berries, melons, coconut, etc.), maple syrup, honey, or even the starch (also a form of sugar) found in vegetables and grains (potatoes, corn, barley, wheat, rye, or rice).

To make vinegar, sugar or starch is first converted to alcohol, which is then fermented into vinegar. Fruit flies are strongly attracted to wine left exposed to open air and act as carriers of *acetobacter*. These bacteria consume and oxidize the alcohol, creating acetic acid. For fermentation to occur, *acetobacter* must be present, oxygen must be present to convert the alcohol, and the temperature must be between 77 and 86° F. Once fermentation has been initiated, *acetobacter* bacteria starts to accumulate on the surface of the vinegar, forming a thin layer that gradually sinks and becomes a gelatinous substance known as "mother of vinegar."

For obvious reasons, winemakers want to prevent acetification. They stop the taps during wine fermentation with a specially designed device that releases any carbon dioxide that has formed in the cask. It also prevents oxygen from entering and keeps out *acetobacter* and other microorganisms that would ruin the wine.

Types of Vinegar

Wine Vinegar

Wine vinegar is made from white, red or rosé wine. If a wine has been granted a certification of *appellation d'origine controllée*, the vinegar can be sold as, for example, a true Burgundy Wine Vinegar or Champagne Vinegar, depending on which wine was used to produce it. A wide variety of ingredients, including *fines herbes*, garlic, chili peppers, flowers, and fruit can be steeped in wine vinegar to make flavored vinegars. These infused vinegars can be used in vinaigrettes and sauces to add nuanced, aromatic flavors.

White wine vinegar with shallots, for example, is excellent in Béarnaise sauce, and chili vinegar makes a superb seasoning for simple seafood dishes. Raspberry vinegar works wonderfully with fatty poultry like duck or goose, while a splash of wine vinegar in marinades helps tenderize meat and poultry, and a dash in stews and sauces adds a subtle tang.

When planning a menu, choose a vinegar that will complement the wine being served at the table. Select red wine vinegar for a poultry sauce paired with a red Bordeaux. Use white wine vinegar to season seafood starters like a crab and shrimp salad served alongside a Muscadet *sur lie*. If Champagne is the beverage of the evening, choose Champagne vinegar for vinaigrettes and sauces.

Reims Vinegar

Reims vinegar is produced from sediment left over after the second fermentation of Champagne. Between 1 ⅓ and 2 tbsp of sediment is removed from each bottle and placed in aerated tanks to be turned into vinegar. The end product contains 7% acetic acid and has a clear amber color, a delicate aroma, and a light, woody flavor. Red and white wine vinegars have existed in Champagne for centuries.

Orleans Vinegar

Orleans vinegar is traditionally made in oak barrels, where wine is introduced to a mother of vinegar culture that has been left in the barrel for one or two generations. The wine is left to ferment anywhere from a few weeks to six months. The resulting vinegar is drawn off, filtered, and bottled. When vinegar is drawn from the casks, about 15% of the vinegar is left in the casks to blend with the next batch, and new wine is added, creating a cycle. The finished unpasteurized vinegar retains a deep aroma and color. Mother of vinegar can sometimes reform in the bottle and can simply be left there, filtered, or even used to start a new bottle of vinegar. Martin-Pouret, a family-run company founded in 1797, is the only vinegar maker to continue to produce vinegar following the Orleans tradition.

Balsamic Vinegar

Although balsamic vinegar only recently became a standard ingredient on supermarket shelves, it has actually been used for hundreds of years. During the Renaissance, it was sent along with romantic letters as a lover's gift, a cherished, precious nectar, often presented in a beautifully etched bottle. Unlike wine, cider, or alcohol vinegars, balsamic vinegar is not made with alcohol, but with the juice of pressed Trebbiano grapes cultivated on the hills bordering Castelvetro in the Modena region of Emilia-Romagna. Grapes are picked as late as possible in autumn when they are bursting with the flavors of sun and earth. Their juice is boiled down until the sugar content is 30% to 50%, then placed in oak barrels to age. Before adding the grape juice, the interior walls of the barrels are coated in vinegar to activate fermentation. The length of time the liquid is left to age, as well as the successive transferring of the vinegar into barrels made of different types of wood — cherry, chestnut, mulberry, acacia, juniper and ash — are what give balsamic vinegar its unique flavor. The alternating hot and cold conditions in which the vinegar is stored further improves its taste. During fermentation, the vinegar is successively placed in smaller and smaller casks. After a minimum of 12 months, the vinegar becomes delicately aromatic. Balsamic vinegar has a dark brown color and a balanced flavor.

To carry the title of *tradizionale*, by law balsamic must be produced according to strict regulations, using grapes from Italy's Modena region. Balsamic can only be marketed as *vecchio* after aging in barrels for 12 years, and can only be called *extra-vecchio* after aging for 25 years or longer. These vinegars are very expensive, and the relatively low quantity of vinegar produced each year (2,650 gallons) as well as high demand only increases its cost. Certain 100 ml bottles can cost over 100 dollars, making it the most expensive vinegar in the world. While it is frequently used to dress salads, balsamic vinegar is often added to dishes such as omelets, risotto, veal cutlets and foie gras to enhance flavor, and is a popular base for sauces.

Sherry Vinegar

Originating in Spain and made from wine produced in the Jerez region of southern Andalusia, sherry vinegar is, much like vintage balsamic vinegar, a delicacy that holds secrets of its own. This delicious condiment echoes the flavor of the *amontillado* wine from which it is made and retains a light alcohol taste. In fact, one of sherry vinegar's main characteristics is its residual alcohol content, which can be up to 3%. The use of Palomina and Tinta grapes gives it a unique taste, and winemakers from the Marco region of Jerez often age their vinegars up to 20 or 30 years. Sherry vinegar is fairly sweet and, when used in vinaigrettes, creates an interesting harmony of flavors, especially when the acidity of another salad ingredient such as citrus needs to be counterbalanced. Adding sherry vinegar to gazpacho, strawberries, or roast pork turns these dishes from simple to sublime!

Banyuls Vinegar

anyuls is a sweet dessert wine made from Grenache grapes grown on ancient vines. These particular grapes are cultivated in terraces on the slopes of the Pyrenees overlooking the Mediterranean, bordering Spain and the plains of Roussillon, in the region of Banyuls-sur-Mer. The traditional Banyuls winemaking process is called *mutage*, in which alcohol is added to must to stop fermentation, preserving the natural sugar of the grapes. The wine is then aged in barrels for as long as possible, or outside in glass bottles exposed to the sun. Banyuls must be matured for a minimum of ten months, and Banyuls Grand Cru for at least 30 months. Aging it in oak barrels for up to five years under the hot Mediterranean sun gives this smooth, full-bodied vinegar a strong flavor with notes of red berries, nuts and licorice. Some varieties have a distinct raspberry or blackberry aroma. It is excellent in marinades, perks up mayonnaises and fish salads, and adds depth to poultry gravies and sauces.

Malt and Beer Vinegars

alt vinegar production begins with the sprouting of barley kernels, which are converted into beer. The resulting vinegar has an assertive, slightly bitter flavor reminiscent of beer, and is a popular condiment in Great Britain and northern Europe. Traditional malt vinegar is nearly colorless and generally used for pickling vegetables like cucumbers and pearl onions. It makes an excellent cooking vinegar, adding kick to fried or grilled fish and zesting up plain French fries. Malt vinegar also marries well with chutneys, ketchups, and fruit compotes. Splash malt vinegar onto fresh cucumber salad to add zip to a traditional summer side dish.

Asian and Rice Vinegars

*J*apanese vinegar is made from fermented sake (rice wine) and is known for its low acidity. The methods for producing sake and rice vinegar are almost identical. Rice vinegar is widely used in Japanese cuisine, and its refined flavor is indispensable to many dishes, including sushi. There are three types of rice vinegar:

- *Kome-zu* is a light rice-based vinegar with a subtle flavor, an essential ingredient in sunomono (vinegared salad).

- *Genmaï-zu* is made from unpolished brown rice, giving it a deeper flavor than kome-zu.

- *Kuro-zu* is a black vinegar. Its distinctive color is obtained by combining steamed rice, koji[8], water, and seed vinegar, and then placing the mixture in jars and allowing it to ferment in the sun for one year. Kuro-zu has a vibrant, full-bodied flavor and is rich in amino acids. Aka-zu, or red vinegar, is an older variety of dark vinegar made with sake lees and aged for three years. It has a pronounced tartness.

Soy sauce, vinegar, and sesame oil are the three main seasonings that have been used in China since ancient times. The Chinese have been fermenting rice and yangmei fruit for 6,000 years. Rice vinegar is made with sour fermented wine; other vinegars are produced by fermenting sorghum, wheat and sweet potatoes. Chinese cuisine, much like the philosophy behind it, ultimately aspires to create perfect balance through precise combinations of colors, flavors, and textures. All Chinese vinegars — white, red, or black, depending on the type of rice used — have strong undertones. Baoning vinegar has been produced in Langzhong since the Yuan (1206-1368) and Ming (1368-1644) dynasties. It has become one of China's most celebrated vinegars because of its quality, unique taste, and various nutritional properties.

---

8   *Koji is an ingredient used to prepare miso, rice vinegar, sake, and amasake.*

Aromatic Zhenjiang vinegar, made from locally grown rice, is a specialty of Eastern China's Jiangsu province and is widely used in Sichuan cuisine. Because it is fermented outdoors, the quality of the vinegar strongly depends on local weather conditions.

Chinese black vinegar is made by fermenting sorghum, wheat, and sweet potatoes. It has a rich but mild flavor that brings out the sweetness in dishes with its light acidity. The vinegar's slight sourness can be used to enhance the flavor of many different dishes or to reduce strong cooking smells, including that of fish.

Apple Cider Vinegar

To start the vinegar-making process, apple cider is produced from fresh apple juice. The juice is placed in barrels; yeast or alcoholic ferment, found naturally in apple seeds or spores when they are picked, is then added. The yeast feeds on the juice's naturally occurring sugars and converts then into alcohol and carbon dioxide (the main components of cider), resulting in an alcohol percentage of 10 to 12%. The hard cider is then placed in a new barrel.

The process of making cider vinegar begins as soon as the cider is put into oak or pine barrels. A viscous substance called mother of vinegar forms on the surface and initiates fermentation. No filtration or pasteurization is required. After fermenting for several weeks, the liquid is poured into bottles made of opaque glass, which blocks light and prevents oxidation. The mother of vinegar remains in the barrel when the vinegar is bottled, but it can gradually reform at the bottom of the bottles once they are stored. This is completely natural and signals that the vinegar is high quality and 100% pure. Mother of Vinegar can be consumed and is highly nutritious.

Unfiltered, unpasteurized apple cider vinegar has many health benefits. It is fortified with approximately 30 essential nutrients, about a dozen minerals, over half a dozen vitamins and amino acids, several enzymes, and a healthy amount of pectin. It is extremely rich in potassium and trace elements such as phosphorus, sulfur, iron, fluoride, calcium, magnesium, silicon, boron, and so on. Cider vinegar is also used for pickling and in stocks for cooking fish and seafood dishes.

Blueberry Vinegar

Blueberry vinegar is made by soaking blueberries in cider vinegar and has an attractive blue tint.

Maple Vinegar

Maple vinegar is made from maple sap and maple syrup. One document from 1913 reveals that at the time, between 25 and 30 gallons of high quality vinegar could be obtained from 1,000 tapped trees. .

At 50 °F, alcoholic fermentation occurs spontaneously in barreled syrup. This is the first step in maple vinegar production. The next step is the addition of one or two yeast tablets or a quantity of raisins. After two weeks fermentation is complete, and the liquid is carefully filtered and combined with a small amount of older vinegar. The barrel is stored at 70 °F to encourage fermentation.

A measure of vinegar equal to $\frac{1}{10}$ of the volume of alcoholic liquid is sometimes added to obtain higher quality vinegar. When making large quantities of vinegar, production is activated by slowly filtering the liquid with clean beechwood chips pre-saturated with hot vinegar to introduce the necessary acetic acid bacteria.

Artisanal maple vinegar is still made today using the traditional method. It is characteristically low in acid but high in flavor — just a few drops are needed to give even the simplest dishes a unique seasoning. Add maple vinegar right before serving to prevent its distinct aroma from evaporating.

Coconut Palm or Toddy Vinegar

Toddy is the sap obtained from cutting the inflorescence[9] or stem of unbloomed coconut palm flowers. This sap is used to make syrup, raw or granulated sugar, fermented beverages, distilled alcohol (arrack[10]), or vinegar. Fresh toddy contains 12 to 15% sugar, similar to the percentage found in cane sugar. It is a milky, whitish, slightly alcoholic liquid also known as palm wine. Toddy vinegar is made by fermenting fresh toddy until it becomes acidic, and it is used to prepare vinegar solutions and to season various dishes. The vinegar is clear, with a clean, smooth, refined flavor.

---

9 *Inflorescence is the flowering part of a plant.*

10 *Arrack (also known as arraki, arack, arak, or raki) is derived from the Arabic work arak, meaning "condensation." There are many different arrack producers as well as many varieties of arrack, and it can also made with rice or palm tree sap. In Greece, for example, it is made from grain, and in the Middle East and in Egypt from dates or grapes.*

Pure White Vinegar

Plain white vinegar is made either by distilling malt vinegar or from a simple mixture of acetic acid and water. Cornstarch (a sugar) is also used as a base. It is fermented and then distilled into a neutral alcohol, which is then fermented into white vinegar.

White vinegar containing 5% acetic acid can be found in most North American pantries. It is used as a condiment, as a cooking and baking ingredient, in salad dressings, mayonnaise, mustard, ketchup, salsa, barbecue sauces, hot sauces, and marinades, and for preserving as well as cleaning.

Vinegar is the best multi-purpose cleaning product available and has been used for centuries to remove stains and soap residue, kill mold, and clear clogged drains and pipes. It is also an extremely effective polishing agent, tartar remover, fabric softener and deodorizer.

Discover New Ways to Cook Delicious Dishes with Flavorful Vinegars

(See Part Three)

Wine Vinegar

Rack of Pork with Pears and Wine Vinegar
p.95

Oysters with White Wine Vinegar and Pastis
p.105

Zesty Citrus Duck Breast
p.130

Marinated Button Mushrooms
p.161

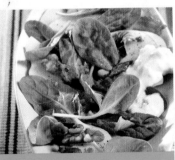

Pear and Spinach Salad
p.176

Balsamic Vinegar

Balsamic-Glazed Pork Loin

p.97

Caramelized Chicken with Peppers

p.118

Mango-Cucumber Summer Salad

p.184

Veal Cutlets with Balsamic and Portobellos

p.143

Pasta with Fennel and Swiss Chard

p.162

Veal Liver with Balsamic and Pine Nuts

p.146

Ricotta-Stuffed Potatoes Au Gratin

p.158

Barbecued Balsamic-Marsala Veal Medallions

p.145

Balsamic-Glazed Sichuan Chicken and Nectarines

p.120

Apple Cider Vinegar

Chicken Salad with Curry Vinaigrette

p.175

Country Salad

p.188

Moroccan Salad

p.190

Sautéed Green Beans

p.156

Penne with Chicken and Peppers

p.126

Mexican Braised Beef

p.139

Pan-Grilled Salmon Steaks with Lime and Dill

p.110

Pork Roast with Cider Vinegar Marinade

p.92

Quick and Easy Baked Trout

p.108

Beet and Endive Salad

p.183

Sherry Vinegar

Beer-Braised
Rabbit with
Prunes

p.129

Zesty
Gazpacho

p.155

Rice Vinegar

Ginger-Garlic
Chicken
Wraps with
Fresh Cilantro

p.123

PART TWO

Practical Guide

Healthy Living with Vinegar

Apothecaries and pharmacists have been using herbs, essential oils and vinegar since ancient times. During the Middle Ages, people relied on different herbs to clean unwholesome air and to repel insects that were believed to spread disease. Dried herbs such as rosemary, thyme and rue were placed alongside roads traveled by royal processions to protect monarchs and their families from disease. To this day, herbs, oils and vinegars are still used for medicinal purposes and should be placed front and center on modern supermarket and drugstore shelves!

Apple Cider Vinegar

Most people are familiar with the adage that an apple a day keeps the doctor away. The pectin in apples has a cleansing effect and helps lower cholesterol levels; the potassium encourages calcium absorption, which helps maintain healthy bone marrow. Apples also contain proteins, carbohydrates, vitamins, three amino acids, minerals, and trace elements including sodium, magnesium and phosphorus in addition to potassium and calcium. For centuries, apple cider vinegar has been used to prevent illness, help relieve the symptoms of respiratory, digestive and intestinal problems, and promote healing. Apple cider vinegar that is 100% pure, unfiltered, and unpasteurized can have extraordinary curative effects and retains all of the nutritional and medicinal properties of fresh apples. The vinegar's natural acidity promotes internal cleansing, eliminates toxins, kills unhealthy bacteria, regenerates intestinal flora, and helps prevent and relieve constipation and flatulence. Unfiltered and unpasteurized apple cider vinegar is extremely rich in trace elements (calcium, sulfur, iron, silicon, boron, phosphorus, magnesium, potassium, and fluoride), pectin, vitamins (especially vitamins B and D), essential acids, enzymes, and essential amino acids. It also contains beta-carotene, which is rich in the antioxidant vitamin A and helps with the absorption of calcium.

Acne

Cider vinegar is a natural astringent and has a pH level very similar to the skin's. Cider vinegar is an excellent remedy for oily and problem skin. It helps clear up teenage acne and occasional breakouts, prevents blackheads, closes pores, and slows the signs of aging thanks to its antioxidant properties. (See Vinegar, A Natural Beauty Product)

Arthritis

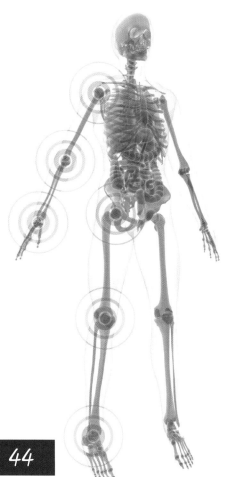

Easing arthritis pain requires balancing the body's acid-base ratio by choosing alkaline foods over acidic ones and introducing minerals into the diet. Cider vinegar can play an important role in minimizing arthritis pain by promoting the softening and elimination of crystals formed in body tissues (chondrocalcinosis). It can also help slow arthritis progression. To help soothe a particularly painful region, apply hot salt water to the affected area and then rub with cider vinegar. Cider vinegar is also used externally for muscle pain and stiffness, inflammation, and sprains by again applying hot salt water to the affected area and rubbing with cider vinegar.

Tonsillitis	Gargle four to six times a day with 2 to 3 tablespoons of cider vinegar mixed with warm water. Drink the remaining mixture.
Asthma	Massage the chest with undiluted vinegar during an asthma attack. If skin is sensitive, mix equal parts vinegar and lavender flower infusion and rub onto the chest.
Anti-Fungal/ Athlete's Foot	Soak feet in a mixture of two parts hot water and one part vinegar and a handful of coarse salt. After soaking, rub feet with shea butter mixed with a few drops of geranium or juniper essential oil and wear a pair of old socks overnight.
Foot Odor	Soak feet in a mixture of two parts hot water and one part vinegar and a handful of coarse salt. The vinegar acts as an antiseptic and deodorant.
Insect Bites and Jellyfish or Nettle Stings	To soothe irritated skin due to spider bites or painful stings from jellyfish, wasps, bees, etc., swab the area immediately with cider or rose vinegar or pour either directly onto the sting or bite. Vinegar can also be used as an inexpensive non-toxic and insecticide-free mosquito repellent.

Vomiting	Apply a compress soaked in warm vinegar to the stomach, repeating whenever the compress becomes cold.
Lice	Rinsing hair with vinegar and water won't kill mature insects, but it will dissolve the shell of the eggs (nits). Preventing the nits from hatching will stop the appearance of any new lice during treatment. To protect the scalp from irritation due to harsh store-bought lice treatments, fill a pot with one-third vinegar and two-thirds water, heat to the highest tolerable temperature and rinse hair with the mixture. Leave in for five to ten minutes and rinse with warm water.
Sunburn and Minor Burns	Rose vinegar, not apple cider vinegar, should be used to treat sunburn and minor burns. Apply a vinegar-soaked compress to the burn or spray vinegar directly onto the affected area.
	Rose Vinegar: Soak a handful of fresh rose petals (ideally pesticide-, fungicide- and insecticide-free) in vinegar for two or three days. Filtered rose vinegar can also be used as a skin cleanser.

Cholesterol and Blood Sugar Control

Apples are naturally rich in pectin, which helps control cholesterol and blood sugar levels. They are also high in cellulose, which promotes intestinal health, and are rich in vitamins A, B_1, B_2, and C, and flavonoids.

Chapped Skin

Avoid using soap, and wash affected areas with vinegar and water instead. After cleansing, apply a mixture of equal parts glycerin, cider vinegar, and burdock. Use daily until skin has fully healed. The mixture will keep for two to three days.

Diabetes

Adding a small amount of vinegar (1 to 2 tablespoons) to high-carbohydrate meals reduces the spike in glucose and insulin concentrations in the blood that occurs 30 to 60 minutes after a meal. The acetic acid in vinegar lowers the blood sugar and insulin levels in the body.

Skin Irritations

Apple cider vinegar helps soothe itchy, irritated skin. Combine 1 tablespoon cornstarch with 1 tablespoon vinegar to make a paste. Apply to the affected area.

Use cider vinegar to help ease the discomfort of pruritis, hives, eczema, psoriasis, and other skin irritations. It also makes an excellent disinfectant, antiseptic, and antibacterial agent. Vinegar and water is often used to treat infections of the ears and face.

Superficial Wounds and Burns

A 50/50 mixture of white vinegar and water makes an ideal disinfectant for superficial wounds and burns.

Acute Dermatitis

Symptoms of acute dermatitis include peeling and 'weeping' blisters. Avoid using soap; instead, combine equal parts cider vinegar, burdock root infusion, and almond oil and use to clean the affected area by gently patting with a compress soaked in the mixture. Let dry and repeat four times a day.

Muscle Pain

Make a homemade balm by whisking together one egg yolk with 1 teaspoon essence of turpentine, 1 tablespoon apple cider vinegar and 1 tablespoon thyme infusion. Massage gently into sore, tight muscles.

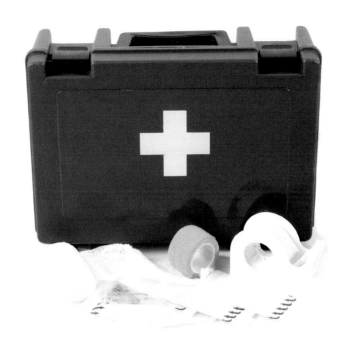

General Good Health

Drink a glass a day of warm water mixed with 1 teaspoon apple cider vinegar and a spoonful of honey.

Sprains

Make a homemade muscle massage balm by whisking together one egg yolk with 1 teaspoon essence of turpentine, 1 tablespoon apple cider vinegar, and 1 tablespoon thyme infusion. Massage gently onto sprained joint.

Cold Intolerance

Build up tolerance to cold weather by following these three simple steps for a few weeks when the weather starts to turn chilly: twice a week, take a bath in hot water to which 4 cups of white vinegar and 2 lbs of sea salt have been added. Shower every morning, alternating between cold and hot water, and then massage the body with vinegar. Try perfumed vinegar for an extra-special massage! After several days, blood circulation will improve and sensitivity to cold will be reduced.

Hiccups

Suck on a sugar cube soaked in apple cider vinegar to cure hiccups!

Urinary Tract Infections

For urinary infections, take 1 tablespoon of apple cider vinegar diluted with water before every meal. Contrary to popular belief, cranberries do not acidify urine. In fact, cranberries prevent bacteria from attaching to the walls of the bladder and the urinary tract. Drink cranberry juice with vitamin C and apple cider vinegar to help speed recovery.

Sore Throat

Soothe a sore throat by gargling with a mixture of 2 tablespoons apple cider vinegar in ⅓ cup of water. Gargle every hour in the morning, and then every two hours in the afternoon.

Headache

Combine one part vinegar and one part steaming hot water. Inhale steam 80 times to help ease headache pain.

Apply a thick compress soaked in a vinegar solution (⅓ vinegar with ⅔ water) to the forehead or to the nape of the neck. Remove once cooled.

Insomnia and Nervousness

Drink 1 or 2 teaspoons of apple cider vinegar in a glass of warm water mixed with honey before bedtime. Take a hot 15- to 20-minute bath with ½ cup of cider vinegar added to regulate nervousness and facilitate sleep, or simply to relax after a long day.

Nausea

Drink 1 teaspoon apple cider vinegar in ¼ cup of sparkling water as soon as symptoms appear. If nausea is due to pregnancy, drink the mixture first thing in the morning. If symptoms occur after meals, drink 1 teaspoon cider vinegar combined with ¼ cup of lemon balm infusion.

Ear Care

Vinegar's high acidity makes it an excellent disinfectant, and it could eventually be used as a possible alternative to antibiotics to help treat external conditions. A recent study shows that a 50/50 solution of vinegar and water is effective in preventing bacterial infections in the ear canal when applied with cotton swabs. It is also effective in preventing external otitis, or swimmer's ear, which often affects frequent swimmers and divers. Simply mix one part vinegar with one part boiled water and rinse ears with the solution after swimming.

Blood Pressure

The acetic acid in vinegar helps lower blood pressure and renin activity. Renin is an enzyme that produces hypertension-causing peptides.

Digestive Problems

Apple cider vinegar helps promote healthy digestion by increasing enzyme levels, killing bad bacteria, and absorbing excess stomach acid, making it an ideal treatment for heartburn, cramps and belching. It also helps stimulate slow digestion, decrease the symptoms of food poisoning, reduce intestinal cramps and gas, and renew intestinal flora. To prevent indigestion, take cider vinegar 30 minutes before eating. If problems occur after eating heavy meals, drink 1 teaspoon cider vinegar in ¼ cup sparkling water.

Constipation

To relieve and prevent constipation, drink 1 teaspoon vinegar in ¼ cup sparkling water before bedtime.

Weight Loss

Apple cider vinegar can also play an important role in weight loss thanks to its high pectin content and rich concentration of powerful enzymes. Vinegar, when incorporated into a healthy eating plan, can help fight obesity and cellulite by destroying excess fat. Combine it with ginger, cayenne pepper, pineapple, citrus fruits (especially grapefruit), or kelp to help with weight loss. Take 2 teaspoons two to three times a day.

Athlete's Foot

Athlete's Foot is a fungal infection of the skin between the toes. Apple cider vinegar helps reduce the symptoms thanks to its antiseptic and astringent properties, and is recommended by the U.S.-based Mayo Clinic as a treatment for athlete's foot.

Soak a disposable makeup remover pad in cider vinegar and apply to affected areas. Spray socks with vinegar and wear overnight.

Mosquito Repellent

- 40 drops lavender essential oil
- 40 drops lemongrass essential oil
- 30 drops peppermint essential oil
- $^4/_5$ cup apple cider vinegar
- $^4/_5$ cup mineral oil

Pour all ingredients into a spray bottle. Cover and shake vigorously. Let sit for four days to let ingredients blend to increase the solution's effectiveness.

Spray on all exposed areas including the face, avoiding contact with the eyes. Use mineral oil instead of other oils, since it is absorbed more slowly.

Colds

For an excellent remedy for colds and chills, mix equal parts apple cider vinegar and water, adding a pinch of cayenne pepper and a spoonful of honey to sweeten. Not recommended for people with digestive issues.

Excess Weight

Taking vinegar with a meal can lead to feeling full sooner, resulting in a reduced calorie intake. A lowered glycemic response and increased feeling of fullness are just a few of the remarkable effects of vinegar used as a condiment.

Vaginitis

Soothe the symptoms of vaginitis by adding 3 cups apple cider vinegar to a warm bath or by douching with 2 tablespoons of vinegar added to 2 cups of water for five days. This is not recommended for pregnant women.

Varicose Veins

Massage the legs in an upward motion towards the heart using a homemade lotion made from ¼ cup red wine and ¾ cup of vinegar. Repeat in the morning and in the evening, and drink 1 teaspoon vinegar in ½ cup water.

Rice Vinegar

Rice vinegar, made from brown rice, has been used for cooking and home remedies for hundreds of years; many ancient recipes using rice vinegar survive to this day. According to the Japanese Food Research Laboratories, brown rice vinegar contains five times more amino acids than vinegar made from sake lees, with 20 amino acids and 16 organic acids. A bottle of rice vinegar — even the very best — should always have a thin layer of sediment at the bottom. In fact, this dark-colored residue is considered the mark of high quality vinegar. Recent research findings show that vinegar helps maintain good health and slows the aging process by preventing the formation of two harmful fat peroxides that damage the body's free radicals and cause cholesterol to accumulate on blood vessel walls.

Tamago-Su or Egg Vinegar

Taking vinegar tonics is an ancient custom in Japan, and one of the country's most potent folk remedies is a simple vinegar-based concoction. Immerse a whole raw egg in a glass of rice vinegar and leave for seven days, until the vinegar has completely dissolved the eggshell, leaving only the thin, soft inner membrane. To prepare Tamago-Su, gently break the membrane and pour its contents into the glass of vinegar. Discard the membrane and stir mixture well. Samurais believed that consuming a small amount of this tonic three times a day would provide energy and strength and ensure a long, healthy life.

Vinegar, A Natural Beauty Product

Vinegar has been used since ancient times as a disinfectant, toner, and perfume, and its benefits are still highly valued today. Aromatic plants and herbs have been used for thousands of years for seasoning food, as well as for medicinal purposes; essential oil is a concentration of a plant's aroma compounds that preserves its distinctive scent and beneficial properties.

Beauty Tips and Tricks

Skin Care

Cider vinegar, a natural astringent, has a pH level very close to the skin's. It is nutrient-rich, and keeps skin soft and healthy. Its antioxidants help slow the skin's natural aging process and minimize the appearance of pores. Cider vinegar removes soap and any calcium and chlorine residue left over from tap water, which may cause tightness and discomfort.

Moisturizer for Normal to Dry Skin

- 3 tbsp olive oil
- 3 tbsp wheat germ oil
- 3 tbsp sunflower oil
- 4 egg yolks
- 3 tbsp cider vinegar

Ingredients should be at room temperature.

Combine oils. Beat egg yolks and slowly pour into oil mixture, stirring gently. Add vinegar and stir. Transfer to a small container and store in the refrigerator.

Use this cream to hydrate the skin. It is important to note that all moisturizers are essentially made to imitate the hydrolipidic film (an emulsion of fat and water) that covers the skin's surface. The fat component forms an oily barrier that prevents water from evaporating from the skin.

Cleanser for Dry Skin

- 1 tbsp oatmeal
- ½ tbsp honey
- ½ tbsp olive oil
- ½ tbsp cider vinegar
- 1 tbsp distilled water

Combine all ingredients and let sit for one to two minutes before using.

Apply to face in a gentle circular motion. Rinse with warm water, followed by cold water. Oatmeal softens and nourishes the skin, and honey acts as an antibacterial cleanser. Apple cider vinegar restores the skin's natural balance.

Soothing Facial Mask for Sensitive Skin

- 1 tbsp cider vinegar
- 3 tbsp water
- 4 tbsp oat flour

Dilute vinegar in water then add oat flour, mixing to create a thick paste.

Apply evenly over the skin and let dry. Rinse with warm water.

Lotion for Normal Skin

- 1 tbsp apple cider vinegar
- Cotton pads

Apply undiluted vinegar to clean, dry skin before putting on makeup.

Toner for Oily, Acne-Prone Skin

- 1 Aspirin (ASA)
- ½ cup (125 ml) vinegar
- ½ cup (125 ml) water

Dissolve aspirin in vinegar and add water.

Vinegar removes dead skin and improves the skin's texture, while aspirin helps clear up acne.

Firming Facial Lotion

- 4 cups carnation petals
- 4 cups apple cider vinegar

Soak petals in vinegar for ten days in a cool, dark place.

Dilute 1 tablespoon of the solution in $^4/_5$ cup water. Pat gently onto face with a cotton pad.

To Restore the Skin's pH

Fill the sink with warm water and add 1 or 2 teaspoons of cider vinegar. Rinse face with vinegared water.

Hair Care

Oily Hair
After-Shampoo Rinse

- 2 drops rosemary (or thyme) essential oil
- 1 tbsp alcohol vinegar
- 4 cups mineral water

Dilute essential oils and alcohol vinegar in mineral water.

Rinse hair with mixture. Rosemary (or thyme) essential oil acts as a natural astringent and absorbs excess sebum. Vinegar seals split ends, leaving hair soft and shiny.

Oily Hair
Essential Oil Rinse

- 1 cup (250 ml) dried yarrow
- 1 cup (250 ml) dried lavender
- 1 cup (250 ml) dried rosemary
- Unfiltered, unpasteurized apple cider vinegar (enough to cover herbs)

Place herbs in an airtight glass jar and add enough vinegar to cover completely. Seal tightly and leave to soak for two weeks in a dry, dark place. Filter and store in a bottle.

After shampooing, rinse hair with 1 tablespoon diluted in 1 cup water.

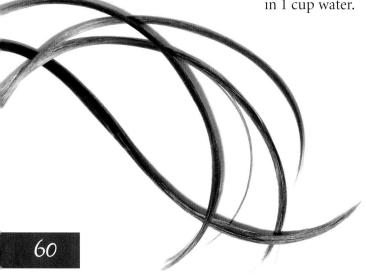

Rinse for Long or Short Hair

- 1 ½ cups (375 ml) cold water, preferably filtered
- 1 tbsp apple cider vinegar
- 4 or 5 drops essential oil (choose essential oil according to hair type and desired effects)
- 4 or 5 drops pure jojoba oil (omit jojoba oil for oily hair)

Combine ingredients in a bowl. After washing hair, wring to remove excess water and place ends in liquid. Thoroughly massage ends, being careful to avoid spilling any liquid. Any oils on the water's surface will be absorbed by the hair. Pour remaining mixture over the head. Do not rinse.

Essential oils to use according to hair type:

- *Normal:* ylang-ylang, lavender, thyme, cedar, rosemary
- *Dry:* sandalwood, sage, geranium
- *Oily:* juniper, rosemary, cedar, lemon, bergamot, grapefruit, cypress, basil, sage, petitgrain, lavender, lemongrass, thyme
- *Dark:* : rosemary
- *Damaged:* tea tree, petitgrain, rosemary, juniper, sandalwood, patchouli

Dry Hair
Aromatic Floral Rinse

- 1 cup (250 ml) dried rose petals
- 1 cup (250 ml) dried chamomile flowers
- 1 cup (250 ml) marshmallow root
- Unfiltered, unpasteurized apple cider vinegar (enough to cover flowers)

Place flowers in an airtight glass jar and add enough vinegar to cover. Seal tightly and leave to soak for two weeks in a dry, dark place. Filter and store in a bottle.

After shampooing, rinse hair with 1 tablespoon mixture diluted in 1 cup water.

Dandruff Rinse

- ½ cup apple cider vinegar

Massage vinegar into hair. Leave for about 20 minutes then rinse. Repeat three or four times a week. Vinegar eliminates dandruff and leaves hair soft and shiny.

To Promote Hair Growth

- 1 lb nettle leaves and roots
- 4 cups vinegar

Soak leaves and roots in vinegar for 15 days in a cool, dark place.
Dilute 2 tablespoons of the solution in 2 cups water. Use after shampooing and conditioning to strengthen hair. Nettle roots, leaves and seeds are extremely effective hair astringents.
Caution: Nettle root may darken hair.

Body Care

Age Spots

- 1 tsp onion juice
- 2 tsp apple cider vinegar
- Cotton pad

Rub mixture into age spots every day until they become noticeably lighter.

Relaxation

- 1 cup (250 ml) apple cider vinegar

Take a hot 15- to 20-minute bath with vinegar added to facilitate sleep, or to simply relax after a long day.

Firming Lotion

- ½ cup (125 ml) lemon balm infusion
- ½ cup (125 ml) eau de Cologne
- ½ cup (125 ml) apple cider vinegar
- ½ cup (125 ml) mineral water

Prepare lemon balm infusion by adding 2 tbsp lemon balm to 4 cups boiling water. Add ½ cup infusion to remaining ingredients.

Rub into skin after showering or bathing. Prepare a new batch every ten days, as it will lose its astringent properties with time. Store in a cool, dark place.

Anti-Cellulite Ivy Bath

• 100 fresh English ivy leaves (hedera helix), chopped
• 1 cup (250 ml) boiling apple cider vinegar

Add chopped ivy leaves to boiling apple cider vinegar. Immediately remove from heat and allow leaves to soak for six hours.

In the bathtub, rub cooled mixture into skin. English ivy contains saponin, a natural cleanser, as well as other cellulite-fighting compounds.

Refreshing After-Sport Lotion

• ½ cup (125 ml) thyme infusion
• ½ cup (125 ml) lavender infusion
• ½ cup (125 ml) apple cider vinegar
• ½ cup (125 ml) boiled water

Prepare thyme infusion by adding 2 tbsp thyme to 4 cups boiling water. Repeat process with lavender for the lavender infusion.

Rub into skin after showering or bathing. Prepare a new batch every ten days, as it will lose its astringent properties. Store in a cool, dark place.

Scented Vinegars

Scented vinegars first appeared around the middle of the 19th century. These vinegar-based blends were usually used in the bath or as a revitalizing lotion. Using scented vinegar to soften water can help strengthen delicate skin and creates a luxurious, deliciously perfumed hot bath. Scented vinegar cleanses, tones, and balances the skin's pH level. Used as a hair care product, it neutralizes the calcium in water, strengthens hair, and leaves it shiny and smooth; it is also an effective treatment for head lice when combined with the regular recommended treatment. Making scented vinegar is easy and requires few materials and ingredients: plants, cheesecloth for filtering, and apple cider vinegar.

Floral Vinegar 1

Use fresh* or dried flowers to prepare this scented vinegar.

- 2 ½ tbsp lavender
- 2 ½ tbsp rosemary
- 2 ½ tbsp rosehip
- 2 ½ tbsp sage
- 2 ½ tbsp carnation petals
- 4 cups apple cider vinegar

*Fresh flowers are more fragrant

Soak mixture for 15 days in a cool, dark place, shaking jar or bottle occasionally to blend ingredients. Filter with cheesecloth and store in an airtight bottle.

Use a mixture of 1 tbsp vinegar and 2 cups water to cleanse the skin. Use undiluted as a perfume.

Floral Vinegar 2

- 2 tsp rose petals
- 2 tsp linden
- 2 tsp chamomilel
- 2 tsp lavender
- 2 tsp hollyhock
- 2 tsp marigold
- 2 cups (500 ml) apple cider vinegar

Soak flowers in vinegar for 21 days. Filter with cheesecloth by thoroughly squeezing out plants. Store in an airtight bottle.

Use a mixture of 1 tbsp vinegar and 2 cups water to cleanse the skin. Use undiluted as a perfume.

Rose Vinegar

- ½ lb dried rose petals
- 4 cups apple cider vinegar

Start by placing ¼ lb rose petals in a jar and covering with vinegar. Seal jar tightly. Leave in the sun for three weeks, then filter. Repeat the process by pouring the first batch of vinegar over the remaining rose petals, resealing the jar, and again leaving in the sun for three weeks. Filter with cheesecloth by thoroughly squeezing out petals. Store in an airtight glass bottle.

Use a mixture of 1 tbsp vinegar and two cups water to cleanse the skin. Use undiluted as a perfume.

Rejuvenating Travel Toner

- ½ cup (125 ml) apple cider vinegar
- 1 tsp 90% alcohol
- 1 tsp fine sea salt
- 4 drops eucalyptus essential oil
- 4 drops galbanum essential oil
- 4 drops nana mint essential oil
- 4 drops geranium essential oil
- 4 drops lavender essential oil

In a pot, reduce the vinegar by half and, once cooled, add alcohol, salt and essential oils. Leave to age in an airtight bottle in a cool, dry place. To obtain a clear amber liquid, filter after three months. Use undiluted as a perfume.

Household Uses for Vinegar

White vinegar is an environmentally friendly and inexpensive antibacterial cleaner. It disinfects, removes odors and stains, cleans glass and mirrors without leaving streaks, and shines and polishes stainless steel, brass, copper, and even leather. The science behind it is simple: vinegar contains a powerful acid that reacts with many organic materials, and because of this it can be used as a safe eco-friendly cleaner. White vinegar is preferred over cooking vinegars as a cleaner because it is colorless and almost odorless.

Use vinegar in the kitchen to kill bacteria, give new life to old pots and pans, shine glasses and porcelain without streaking, and clean the oven without backbreaking scrubbing. Use it in the bathroom to keep the shower scum-free, prevent and attack mold, destroy odors, and clean glass windows and doors. In the bedroom, vinegar refreshes, deodorizes, and cleans surfaces. In the garden, backyard and garage, use vinegar as a natural insecticide, to protect plants from harmful ants, promote plant growth, and even clean the barbecue. For indoor and outdoor pets, use vinegar to eliminate odors, stop itching, and remove hair from furniture and fabric. White vinegar is a household must-have!

All-Purpose Cleaner

- Store in a spray bottle.
- In the spray bottle, mix 1 tbsp baking soda with 3 cups water.

In a glass, combine the following ingredients:

- ½ tbsp white vinegar
- 1 tbsp tea tree essential oil
- 1 tbsp peppermint essential oil

Pour into spray bottle using a funnel and mix well.

Make large batches of this inexpensive cleaner and store in a clean, reusable, labeled container.

Tea tree oil is a powerful antibacterial, while peppermint oil is both antibacterial and antifungal and leaves behind a refreshing minty scent. For lemon-scented or pine-scented cleaner, use 40 drops citronella essential oil, 2 tsp lemon oil, or 40 drops pine oil instead of peppermint oil. Replace the peppermint oil with 1 tsp lavender essential oil to fill any room with the exquisite perfume of Provence!

Window and Glass Cleaner

- 1 cup (250 ml) white vinegar
- 8 drops citronella essential oil
- 8 drops peppermint oil
- ½ cup (125 ml) water

Combine in a spray bottle and use on windows.

Citronella and vinegar are both excellent insect repellents!

Using Newspapers to Clean Windows

Wash windows with a sponge and soapy water and dry with a clean cloth. Spray with vinegar and water and wipe with newspaper for streak-free shine. Keep a cloth handy to wipe away ink smudges on lighter-colored window frames.

Stovetop Cleaner

Combine 3 tbsp baking soda and 1 tbsp water.

Use paste and a vinegar-soaked cloth to clean stovetop.

Oven Cleaner

Combine 1 cup (250 ml) baking soda and ¼ cup (60 ml) sodium carbonate (washing soda).

Wipe the oven's interior with a wet cloth and apply mixture to stains and spots. Leave for several hours.

Scrub with a vinegar-soaked cloth and rinse thoroughly.

Refrigerator and Freezer Cleaner

• Add 1 tsp all-purpose cleaner to hot vinegar or lemon juice.

Thoroughly clean refrigerator walls, drawers, shelves, and doors twice a month for regular upkeep.

Dishwasher Cleaner 1

• Pure vinegar

To remove grease and oil, pour a small amount of white vinegar into the dishwasher along with regular detergent.

Dishwasher Cleaner 2

- ¾ cup (180 ml) bleach
- 2 cups (500 ml) white vinegar

To remove calcium buildup, pour bleach into an empty dishwasher during the first cycle. Add vinegar during the rinse cycle, and then run a second full cycle using regular dishwasher detergent to clear away any residue.

Glassware in the Dishwasher

- ½ cup (125 ml) bleach
- ½ cup (125 ml) white vinegar

Pour bleach into dishwasher during the wash cycle, and then add vinegar during the rinse cycle.

Vinegar will neutralize the bleach and help remove soap scum and streaks on glassware.

Lime and Tartar Remover for Kettles, Irons, and Coffee Pots

- Equal quantities vinegar and water

Add mixture to appliance and bring to a boil to remove mineral buildup.

Lime and Tartar Remover for Coffee Makers

• Fill water reservoir $^4/_5$ full with water and the remaining $^1/_5$ with vinegar.

Brew until coffee pot is half-full and let sit for 15 minutes. Finish brewing cycle, turn off machine, and let sit for another 15 minutes.

Rinse by running one or two brewing cycles with plain water.

Lime Remover for Clothing Irons

• Blend of ¼ vinegar and ¾ water

Fill water reservoir with vinegar and water mixture.

Allow to heat up and release steam until empty.

Rust Spot Remover for Stainless Steel Sinks

• White vinegar and salt paste
• Pure white vinegar

Cover rust spot with a vinegar-soaked cloth and let sit for 30 minutes. Scrub with salt and vinegar paste.

Coffee and Tea Stain Remover for Porcelain

• White vinegar and salt paste

To remove stains, scrub spot with vinegar and salt paste. If stains are particularly stubborn, first soak china in a concentrated blend of baking soda and water and then scrub with paste.

Cooking Odor Eliminator

Simmer equal parts white vinegar and water with a few cloves, bay leaves or lemon zest to get rid of cooking odors.

Cleaner for Burnt Pots and Pans

• 2 tbsp each baking soda and white vinegar

Immediately add vinegar and salt and let soak. If bottom is still burnt, boil water with baking soda and vinegar in pot or pan for 10 minutes.

Pot and Pan Cleaner

Soak pot or pan overnight with water and vinegar.

Calcium Remover for Coffee Pots

- Coarse salt
- 2 cups (500 ml) white vinegar

Add three handfuls coarse salt to 2 cups vinegar in the coffee pot.

Shake well and let sit. Rinse with hot water.

All-Purpose Metal Polish

- Salt, flour and vinegar

Make a paste with salt, flour and vinegar.

Use a cloth to gently polish metal with paste. Rinse with very hot water, then buff until shiny.

Brass and Copper Polish

- White vinegar and salt

Polish with a paste of equal parts salt and white vinegar.

Rinse with very hot water, then buff until shiny.

Stainless Steel Polish

- White vinegar

Wash stainless steel with hot, soapy water and polish with a vinegar-soaked cloth.

Carpets

- ¼ cup (60 ml) white vinegar diluted in 4 cups hot water

To remove stains, gently rub spot with a cloth or brush soaked in vinegar and water mixture. Most stains can be removed with these two basic ingredients. Always rub from the outside in to avoid spreading the stain.

To clean, deodorize and keep carpets and furniture made from synthetic materials looking brand new, always remove stains before they set using a clean cloth or paper towel soaked in vinegar and water.

For food stains, first remove spilled food, then sprinkle with cornstarch or baking soda to absorb liquid and grease. Allow to dry, then use a vacuum or brush to remove excess powder. Sponge stain with a solution of equal parts vinegar and water.

Wood Furniture

- 5 tbsp white vinegar
- 5 tbsp olive oil
- 15 drops lemon essential oil

Use a spray bottle to mist furniture surfaces with the solution. Rub in with a soft cloth. For the best results, heat mixture before using.

Mold

• White vinegar

Wipe down moldy surfaces (like shower curtains and window frames) with vinegar. Allow to evaporate, but do not rinse. Repeat occasionally to prevent the growth of more mold.

Lime and Soap Scum Remover for Shower Doors

• White vinegar

Wipe doors with a hot vinegar-soaked sponge.

Calcium Remover for Tiles

• White vinegar

To get rid of stubborn calcium buildup on ceramic tiles, cover area with a vinegar-soaked cloth or paper towel. Let sit for a few minutes to a few hours, then wipe and rinse with water.

Lime Remover for Taps and Shower Heads

• White vinegar

Frequently wipe down taps and shower heads with vinegar over a period of 1 hour to remove lime, then use an old toothbrush and baking soda to scrub any hard-to-reach buildup.

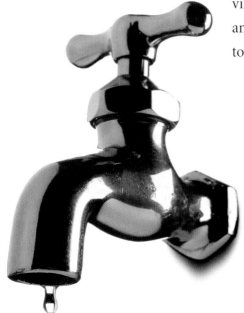

Toilet Cleaner

- 2 cups (500 ml) white vinegar
- ½ cup (125 ml) water
- 2 tsp tea tree essential oil
  or grapefruit essential oil
  or lemon essential oil
  or Douglas pine essential oil
  or eucalyptus essential oil

Combine all ingredients in a spray bottle.

Spray interior and exterior of toilet and leave for 15 to 20 minutes, then scrub.

Toilet Stains

- 2 to 3 tbsp baking soda
- 2 to 3 tbsp fine salt
- ¾ cup (180 ml) white vinegar
- ¾ cup (180 ml) boiling water

Combine ingredients and pour into toilet bowl.

Scrub with toilet brush, leave to soak, and scrub again. If stains are very stubborn, add pure vinegar to toilet water, soak overnight, and then scrub vigorously. Do not use metal brushes on porcelain.

In the Laundry Room

Laundry Detergent

• White vinegar

A mixture of vinegar and water, lemon juice or undiluted vinegar is just as effective as bleach, and won't damage clothes or harm the environment.

White vinegar brightens whites and colors, removes sweat stains and dirt, and softens and freshens laundry. Hydrogen peroxide can be used to remove stubborn stains, but it is important to read clothing labels before using any bleaching or whitening agent.

Fabric Softener

• ¾ cup (180ml) vinegar
• 10 to 12 drops lavender essential oil

Add mixture to rinse cycle.

Ironing Water

Mix 4 cups demineralized water with 1 tsp white vinegar and 15 to 20 drops lavender or lavandin essential oil.

Store in a spray bottle and shake well before each use.

Spray on clothes immediately before ironing.

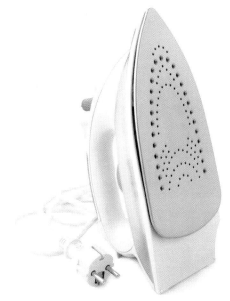

Static Cling Reducer

• ¼ cup (60 ml) to ½ cup (125 ml) white vinegar

Add vinegar to rinse cycle and, if possible, hang items to dry instead of using the dryer.

Colors

Add ½ cup (125 ml) vinegar to a basin of water.

Soak colors in a vinegar and water solution to keep colors bright and prevent them from running and dyeing other articles.

Sweat Stains

• White vinegar

Before washing, soak underarms of shirt or sweater in white vinegar, let sit, and then wash as usual.

White vinegar removes body odor from all fabrics, especially lycra.

Weeds

• White vinegar

Use white vinegar to destroy weeds growing between bricks or in sidewalk cracks. Simply spray weeds with vinegar, avoiding healthy plants.

Ants

• White vinegar

Spray vinegar around doors and areas where ants usually gather. If a colony has infested the sugar bowl or the cupboards, clean the floor, counters, and kitchen appliances with vinegar.

Cats

• White vinegar

To keep cats out of certain areas in the garden or yard, spray these areas with vinegar. White vinegar is also effective at destroying the odor of cat urine — just wipe the area with vinegar after cleaning the mess.

Pet Fleas

• ½ cup (125 ml) apple cider vinegar
• ½ tsp tea tree essential oil
• 1 tsp lavender essential oil

Shake well.

Wipe area twice a day with a cotton ball soaked in the solution.

Cut Flowers

• 2 tsp vinegar
• 1 tsp sugar
• 1 cup (250 ml) water

Place flowers in this mixture to keep them fresh longer.

Calcium Buildup in Pots

• 1 part white vinegar to 7 parts water

Soak terracotta pots for 24 hours and then rinse with water to remove calcium buildup.

Lettuce

• A few drops of white vinegar

To get rid of insects, wash lettuce with water mixed with a few drops of vinegar.

Other Uses

Vomit

- 1 part white vinegar to 1 part sparkling or mineral water

Mix well.

To remove stains (cat urine, vomit, etc.) from carpets, fabric sofas or other stained fabrics, sponge solution onto area, let sit for one minute, and scrub gently.

Boots

- White vinegar

Clean boots with vinegar every night or at least once a week if they are worn every day.

Wipe with a warm cloth to remove excess dirt and mud. Remove salt stains from winter boots by wiping them with a vinegar-soaked sponge. Never use hot water or soap. Apply vinegar generously to leather, scrub gently, then wipe with a dry cloth and let dry away from heat.

Plumbing

- 1 cup (250 ml) baking soda
- 1 cup (250 ml) fine salt

Combine baking soda and salt.

Pour 3 tbsp into the drain and then add boiling vinegar and water solution (⅓ vinegar and ⅔ water).

Jewelry

• 1 part milk to 1 part vinegar

Soak chains or other detailed and delicate pieces of jewelry in the solution. Wash with hot soapy water and polish to dry.

Paintbrushes

• White vinegar

To remove dried, stuck-on paint from paintbrushes, soak in boiling white vinegar. After soaking, bristles will be clean and soft.

PART 3

Delicious Recipes

Consult this legend for the level of difficulty and the health benefits of these recipes:

Difficulty:

X1: Easy

X2: Medium

X3: Hard

X4: Very hard
        Requires preparation in advance

Health benefits:

More ♡ mean the recipe will better suit health and wellness plans

Pork

Apple Cider-Glazed Ham

*A traditional recipe that brings the earthy,
comforting flavors of apple and maple to the table.*

DIFFICULTY |

HEALTH BENEFITS |

Prep time — 10 minutes

Cook time — 2 hours

Ingredients
Serves 6 to 8

- 5 lb boneless or bone-in half ham
- 2 cups (500 ml) apple juice
- 1 cup (250 ml) real maple syrup
- Pepper
- 7 or 8 whole cloves, to taste
- ½ tsp ground cloves
- 1 tsp mustard seeds
- 1 tsp ground ginger
- ¼ cup (60 ml) apple cider vinegar

Preparation

- Place ham in a large saucepan, filling pan with cold water until the ham is half submerged. Add apple juice, ½ cup maple syrup, pepper, whole and ground cloves, mustard seeds, and ½ tsp ginger.

- Bring to a boil over medium heat, then let simmer over low heat for 30 to 40 minutes.

- Preheat oven to 275°F. Put ham into a roasting pan, add remaining ingredients to left over maple syrup, and pour over ham.

- Roast in the oven for approximately 90 minutes, or until ham reaches an internal temperature of 140°F, basting frequently. Add a bit of water if the glaze becomes too thick or starts to caramelize.

- Serve hot, sliced thin. Pour sauce over each serving.

Pork Roast with Cider Vinegar Marinade

*A simple yet delectable parsley and garlic seasoning
brings out the delicate taste of apple cider vinegar.*

DIFFICULTY |

HEALTH BENEFITS | ♡ ♡ ♡

Marinating time	12 hours
Prep time	30 minutes
Cook time	70 minutes

Ingredients

Serves 6

• 2 carrots, finely chopped

• 4 shallots, minced

• 2 cloves garlic, minced

• 1 bunch fresh parsley, finely chopped

• 2 cups (500 ml) cider vinegar

• 3 bay leaves

• 1 sprig of thyme

• Salt and freshly ground pepper

• 4 ½ lb pork roast

• 1 cup (250 ml) tomato puree

Preparation

• Place carrots, shallots, garlic, and parsley in a shallow dish.

• Add cider vinegar, bay leaves, and thyme, and salt and pepper to taste. Place roast in dish and cover with mixture.

• Marinate for 24 hours in the refrigerator, turning approximately every 2 hours.

• Remove roast and vegetables from the marinade, drain well, and place in a roasting pan.

• Bake in a 400°F oven. Baste with drippings after 20 minutes, then lower oven temperature to 300°F. Cook for 40 more minutes, turning roast regularly.

• Pour tomato puree over roast, cover and allow to simmer gently for 10 minutes.

• Serve with puréed vegetables, cabbage or cooked carrots. Use drippings to make a flavorful sauce.

Pork is an excellent source of protein. One ¼ lb serving of cooked pork provides over 25 g of protein, and is rich in vitamins B_1, B_3, B_6, and B_{12}, iron, potassium, phosphorus, copper, manganese, magnesium, selenium, and trace elements that are essential to staying healthy.

Pork with Pears and Vinegar

*The delicate sweetness of pears marries with vinegar
and juniper for incredibly juicy pork.*

Prep time	10 minutes
Cook time	1 hour
Rest time	10 minutes

Difficulty |

Health Benefits | ♡ ♡ ♡

Ingredients

Serves 4

- 3 tbsp olive oil
- 2 ½ lb pork loin
- Salt and pepper
- 4 firm, juicy Bosc pears (or any variety)
- ½ cup (125 ml) white wine or white balsamic vinegar
- 1 tsp allspice
- 1 tsp juniper berries, crushed
- 5 sage leaves
- 1 tbsp butter

Preparation

- Heat oil in a large Dutch oven with a heavy base. Sear pork for 2 minutes over fairly high heat. Add salt and pepper, then lower heat and continue to brown for 8 minutes.

- Peel pears while waiting for meat to brown, removing core and seeds. Cut into quarters.

- Pour vinegar over pork. Once vinegar has evaporated, add pears, allspice, crushed juniper berries, and crumbled sage.

- Cover and cook gently for 45 minutes, turning pork and pears occasionally.

- Remove meat and pears from pan and skim fat from pan juices with a slotted spoon.

- Let pork rest on a plate for 10 minutes and pour jus from resting plate back into Dutch oven with remaining jus. Bring to a boil, add butter, and simmer until slightly thickened, about one minute.

- Slice pork loin and serve with sauce and pears.

Balsamic-Glazed Pork Tenderloin

Honey and balsamic vinegar make a delicious glaze
for tender, flavorful pork tenderloin.

DIFFICULTY |

HEALTH BENEFITS | ♡ ♡ ♡

Prep time	15 minutes
Marinating time	1 hour
Cook time	18 to 20 minutes
Rest time	5 minutes

Ingredients

Serves 6

- 2 tbsp liquid honey
- 2 tbsp wholegrain mustard (Meaux mustard)
- 2 tbsp balsamic vinegar
- 1 tbsp olive oil
- 1 clove garlic, minced
- 1 pinch salt
- 1 pinch pepper
- 2 pork loins, trimmed of fat

Preparation

- In a shallow dish, whisk together honey, wholegrain mustard, balsamic vinegar, olive oil, minced garlic, salt, and pepper. Place pork loins in the dish and coat well with marinade, then cover with plastic wrap.

- Marinate for at least 1 hour, for up to 24 hours.

- Preheat gas barbecue to medium-high. Remove pork from marinade; set marinade aside. Place pork on an oiled grill and brush with remaining marinade. Cover and cook, turning occasionally, for 18 to 20 minutes or until pork is golden brown outside and still slightly pink inside.

- Transfer meat to a cutting board, cover with aluminum foil, and let rest for 5 minutes. Slice pork into ½-inch thick slices using a sharp knife and serve with roasted potatoes and a green vegetable.

This pork is delicious barbecued or pan-grilled. The honey in the sweet-and-sour marinade caramelizes during cooking, giving the meat an intensely flavored crust.

White Balsamic Pork Vindaloo

Cette recette aux notes indiennes est inspirée par le mélange d'épices, les parfums du balsamique blanc et de la coriandre.

DIFFICULTY |

HEALTH BENEFITS | ♡ ♡ ♡ ♡ ♡

Prep time   20 minutes

Marinating time   1 hour minimum

Cook time   2 hours

Preparation

- Place cubed pork in a large bowl. Grind spices with a mortar and pestle, and then add vinegar. Toss meat to coat with spice and vinegar blend. Cover with plastic wrap and marinate in the refrigerator for at least 1 hour.

- Heat olive oil in a Dutch oven and sauté onions and garlic together until onions are soft and translucent. Add tomato paste, meat, and marinade. Cover and cook over low heat for around 2 hours, or until meat is tender and cooked through.

- If necessary, add a bit of water or chicken stock to prevent meat from drying out during cooking. Stir occasionally.

- Remove pot from heat and add chopped cilantro. Serve immediately with basmati rice.

Ingredients

Serves 6

- 1 ¾ lbs pork shoulder, cubed
- 1 bay leaf
- 4 cloves
- 1 cinnamon stick
- 1 tsp peppercorns
- 1 tsp dry mustard
- 1 tsp ground ginger
- 1 tsp mild paprika
- 1 tsp saffron
- ½ tsp turmeric
- 1 tsp curry powder
- ½ tsp crushed chilis
- Salt and freshly ground pepper
- ½ cup (125 ml) white balsamic vinegar
- 1 large onion, chopped
- 4 cloves garlic, minced
- 3 tbsp tomato paste
- 5 tbsp olive oil
- Fresh cilantro, chopped
- Water or chicken stock

Fish & Seafood

Oysters with Fresh Cilantro and Rice Vinegar

Cilantro adds zip to fresh oysters,
creating a perfect balance between East and West.

DIFFICULTY |

HEALTH BENEFITS | ♡ ♡ ♡ ♡ ♡

Prep time   5 minutes

Marinating time   1 hour

Preparation

- Combine all ingredients (except oysters) in a bowl and chill for 1 hour to allow flavors to mingle.
- Garnish oysters and serve.

Ingredients

- 1 shallot, minced
- 1-inch piece ginger root, minced
- ½ English cucumber, peeled and finely chopped
- ½ bunch fresh cilantro, chopped
- 1 cup (250 ml) rice wine vinegar
- Freshly ground pepper
- 48 oysters

Vinegar and oysters are a natural pairing, and their flavors complement and enhance each other when properly matched. Oysters are a source of vitamins, iron, and copper, and are especially rich in iodine and vitamin B_{12}. Depending on the size of the oysters, one serving is usually six to eight as an appetizer, or double that quantity as a main course.

Oysters with White Wine Vinegar and Pastis

Savor the warmth of the sun in Southern France with this Provence-inspired dish!

DIFFICULTY |

HEALTH BENEFITS | ♡ ♡ ♡ ♡ ♡

Prep time   5 minutes

Present oysters on a bed of coarse salt spread over an attractive serving dish to prevent them from sliding around and losing any garnish!

Ingredients

- 4 tbsp dry white wine
- 4 tbsp white wine vinegar
- 2 tbsp pastis
- 1 shallot, minced
- 24 oysters

Preparation

- Combine ingredients and spoon a small amount onto each oyster.
- Serve immediately.

Oysters with Champagne Vinegar

These oysters give Champagne vinegar a well-deserved chance to shine, and will entice even the most hard-to-please palates.

DIFFICULTY |

HEALTH BENEFITS | ♡ ♡ ♡

Cook time	2 minutes
Wait time	25 minutes

Ingredients

- 12 large oysters

For Vinaigrette

- 1 tbsp Champagne vinegar
- 1 tbsp shallots, minced
- Pinch of sugar
- Freshly ground black pepper
- A few sprigs Italian parsley, chopped

For Gratin

- Unsalted butter

For Garnish

- Fresh, finely chopped currants or seedless red grapes

Preparation

- Combine vinaigrette ingredients and let flavors blend for 25 minutes.

- While waiting for vinaigrette, add a pat of unsalted butter to each oyster and broil for 1 to 2 minutes.

- Add parsley to vinaigrette and spoon a small amount onto each oyster. Garnish with currants or grapes to add sweetness and balance the acid in the vinegar.

- Serve immediately.

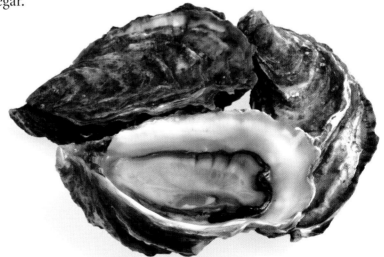

Oysters with Soy Sauce and Balsamic Vinegar

A slightly acidic dressing of soy and balsamic with green onion draws out the subtle flavor of these oysters.

DIFFICULTY |

HEALTH BENEFITS | ♡ ♡ ♡ ♡ ♡

Prep time   5 minutes

Preparation

- Combine ingredients and spoon a small amount into each oyster.

Ingredients

- 4 tbsp balsamic vinegar
- 4 tbsp soy sauce
- 4 tbsp lemon juice
- ½ red pepper, cut into small dice
- 2 green onions, finely chopped
- Pinch of sugar
- Freshly ground black pepper
- 24 oysters

Different Varieties of Oysters

Long Island in New York State is famous for its Blue Point oysters, which have a rounded end and a smooth, meaty texture.

New Brunswick, Canada cultivates BeauSoleil oysters and Caraquet oysters. BeauSoleils are rounded or oblong and sand-free, with a delicate taste and firm flesh, while Caraquets are meatier, with a fresh, briny flavor.

Malpeque oysters from Prince Edward Island, Canada, are light-bodied and saltier with a silky texture. PEI Raspberry Point oysters have a nicely rounded flavor with a sweet, lingering finish. South Lake oysters are known for their salty, juicy meat.

Quick and Easy Baked Trout

*The delicately mild taste of trout marries perfectly with vinegar
and tarragon for a delectable meal in no time at all!*

DIFFICULTY |

HEALTH BENEFITS | ♡ ♡ ♡ ♡

Trout is rich in omega-3 fatty acids as well as vitamins, iron, and trace elements.

Prep time   5 minutes

Cook time   25 minutes

Preparation

- Place trout fillets on a large sheet of oiled aluminum foil.

- Cover fish with remaining ingredients and seal foil tightly. Wrap in another piece of foil.

- Cook in a 350°F oven for 30 minutes.

Ingredients
Serves 2

- 2 trout fillets

- 1 onion, quartered

- 1 green pepper, julienned

- 1 tsp tarragon

- 2 tbsp apple cider vinegar

- Garlic salt

- Pepper

Pan-Grilled Salmon Steaks with Lime and Dill

This elegant dish features the classic pairing of dill and salmon with a twist – a zippy marinade of lime and apple cider vinegar!

DIFFICULTY |

HEALTH BENEFITS | ♡ ♡ ♡ ♡ ♡

Prep time	10 minutes
Marinating time	1 hour
Cook time	8 to 10 minutes

Ingredients

Serves 4

- ⅓ cup (80 ml) olive oil
- 2 tbsp apple cider vinegar
- ½ tsp garlic juice
- Juice of ½ lime
- Zest of 1 lime
- ½ tsp cayenne pepper
- ½ tsp black pepper
- ½ tsp sea salt
- ½ tsp dill
- 4 salmon steaks

Preparation

- In a bowl, combine half of the oil with all of the vinegar, garlic juice, lime juice, lime zest, cayenne pepper, black pepper, salt, and dill.

- In a shallow dish, coat salmon steaks with marinade and chill for 1 hour in the fridge.

- In a non-stick pan, heat the remaining oil and grill for 4 to 5 minutes per side, depending on the thickness of the steaks.

Salmon is extremely rich in omega-3, a fatty acid that helps maintain a healthy cardiovascular system. It is also high in vitamins A and D, as well as magnesium.

Salmon with Maple Vinegar

Pamper your taste buds with a rich, warming salmon dish infused with the flavors of maple and whiskey and topped with an elegant caviar garnish.

DIFFICULTY |

HEALTH BENEFITS | ♡ ♡ ♡ ♡

Prep time	30 minutes
Cook time	10 minutes

Ingredients
Serves 4

For sauce

- 10 black peppercorns
- 4 tbsp maple vinegar or 3 tbsp white vinegar and 1 tbsp pure maple syrup
- 4 tbsp dry white wine
- 4 tbsp 35% cream
- ½ cup (125 ml) cold butter
- A few chives, chopped

For salmon

- 4 skinless salmon fillets
- 1 pinch salt
- 1 tbsp whiskey (optional)
- 1 tbsp maple or brown sugar
- 1 tbsp salmon or trout caviar
- A few whole chives

Preparation

For sauce

- In a saucepan, add whole peppercorns to maple vinegar and white wine and reduce until only 2 tbsp remain.

- Add cream and bring to a boil. Incorporate butter by whisking small pieces into sauce one at a time until melted and sauce is completely smooth. Remove peppercorns, add chopped chives, and keep warm.

For salmon

- Lightly salt fillets, brush with whiskey, and sprinkle with maple or brown sugar.

- Cook in an unoiled non-stick pan for 5 minutes, turning often. Add more salt.

- Ladle a spoonful of sauce onto each plate and arrange salmon on top. Garnish with caviar and whole chives.

Poultry & Game

Chicken with Oregano and Olives

Roasting the chicken slowly allows it to soak up this intensely vibrant Mediterranean-inspired marinade.

DIFFICULTY |

HEALTH BENEFITS | ♡ ♡ ♡ ♡ ♡

Prep time	10 minutes
Marinating time	3 hours
Cook time	1 hour

Ingredients
Serves 6

- 2 chicken breasts and 6 chicken thighs
- ⅓ cup (80 ml) apple cider vinegar
- 1 small can stewed tomatoes
- 2 green peppers, chopped into large pieces
- 1 onion, chopped
- 1 clove garlic, minced
- 1 tsp oregano
- 1 tsp thyme
- Salt and freshly ground pepper
- ⅓ cup (80 ml) olive oil
- 20 green olives

Preparation

- In a Dutch oven, combine chicken, vinegar, tomatoes, peppers, onion, garlic, herbs, and salt and pepper.

- Marinate for 3 hours in the refrigerator.

- Remove chicken, wipe off marinade, and brown in olive oil. Transfer back to Dutch oven.

- Add olives, cover and cook in a 350°F oven for 1 hour.

Chicken is an excellent source of protein, niacin, vitamin B₅, iron, zinc, phosphorus, and amino acids. Cooked or raw red, yellow, or green peppers are an excellent source of vitamin C and vitamin A, and a good source of potassium. They also contain vitamin B₆ and folic acid. Garlic is a well-known antioxidant, and a natural source of nutrients, potassium, sulphur, and trace elements.

117

Caramelized Chicken and Peppers

This chicken becomes wonderfully caramelized and boasts a heavenly fragrance of spices, while the balsamic vinegar highlights the fresh peppers.

DIFFICULTY |

HEALTH BENEFITS |

| Prep time | 30 minutes |
| Cook time | 1 hour 10 minutes |

Ingredients
Serves 6

- Salt and freshly ground black pepper
- 1 large chicken, cut into pieces, or 6 thighs
- 2 tbsp olive oil
- 6 peppers (3 red and 3 yellow)
- 4 to 6 cloves garlic
- 2 tbsp sugar
- 2 tsp cumin
- 1 tsp paprika
- 1 pinch ground Espelette pepper or cayenne pepper
- 2 tsp oregano
- 1 or 2 tbsp balsamic vinegar
- 24 black olives
- A few fresh basil leaves

Preparation

- Salt and pepper chicken pieces. In a skillet, add olive oil and brown chicken over high heat for 5 minutes on each side.

- While chicken is browning, wash peppers, remove stem and seeds, and chop each one into 8 long strips. Peel garlic and roughly chop.

- When chicken is golden brown, transfer to a plate and sauté peppers and garlic in the same skillet for 10 minutes, stirring often.

- Add sugar, salt, pepper, cumin, paprika, ground Espelette or cayenne, and oregano, and let caramelize for 10 minutes.

- Pour in vinegar and add chicken back to skillet. Stir well, cover, and cook 30 minutes over low heat.

- After 30 minutes, add olives and cook another 10 minutes.

- Sprinkle with fresh basil before serving.

Balsamic-Glazed Sichuan Chicken and Nectarines

Balsamic vinegar and nectarines carry this dish to new heights by adding a fragrant, summery touch of sweetness!

DIFFICULTY |

HEALTH BENEFITS | ♡ ♡ ♡ ♡

Prep time	10 minutes
Marinating time	1 hour
Cook time	20 minutes

Ingredients

Serves 4

- 4 chicken breasts
- 3 tbsp balsamic vinegar
- 2 tbsp olive oil
- Sea salt
- Sichuan pepper, ground
- 4 nectarines
- Wooden skewers

Preparation

- Cut chicken breasts into equal-sized pieces. In a shallow dish, toss to coat with vinegar, olive oil, salt, and pepper.

- Cover and marinate in refrigerator for 1 hour.

- Preheat oven to 425°F.

- Gently wash nectarines, remove pits, and cut into quarters.

- Tightly thread marinated chicken and nectarine quarters alternately onto skewers that have been soaked in water for 30 minutes.

- Generously sprinkle with salt and pepper and bake for approximately 20 minutes, turning and adding the remaining marinade halfway through cooking.

Ginger-Garlic Chicken Wraps with Fresh Cilantro

Serve these fresh wraps hot or cold as a deliciously simple Asian-inspired main course or as a tasty protein-packed snack.

DIFFICULTY |

HEALTH BENEFITS | ♡ ♡ ♡ ♡

Prep time   30 minutes

Cook time   10 minutes

Dark meat, (like chicken thigh meat) results in a more tender, succulent filling.

Ingredients
Serves 3

- 2 tbsp vegetable oil
- ½ cup (125 ml) sesame seeds
- ½ cup (125 ml) pine nuts
- 1 ½ lbs chicken, thinly sliced
- 4 tbsp garlic, minced
- 4 tbsp ginger, minced
- 2 tbsp soy sauce
- ½ cup (125 ml) chili sauce
- ⅔ cup (160 ml) rice vinegar
- 1 bunch fresh cilantro
- Pitas, tortillas or lettuce for wrapping

Preparation

- In a pan, heat oil and brown sesame seeds and pine nuts over high heat for about 2 minutes until golden.

- Add chicken, garlic, and ginger. Cook until chicken is golden brown.

- Add soy sauce, chili sauce, and rice vinegar.

- Sauté over medium heat for 2 minutes. Add chopped cilantro.

- Serve wrapped in pitas, tortillas or lettuce.

Balsamic-Grilled Chicken with Sea Salt

The perfect dish for a summer barbecue or a cozy winter meal
– a hit with kids and adults alike!

DIFFICULTY |

HEALTH BENEFITS |

Prep time   10 minutes
Cook time   60 minutes

Ingredients
Serves 4

- 3 tbsp olive oil
- 3 tbsp balsamic vinegar
- 1 pinch dried oregano
- 1 pinch coarse sea salt or fleur de sel
- Freshly ground pepper
- 8 chicken drumsticks
- Wooden skewers
- ¾ cup (180 ml) water

Preparation

- Preheat barbecue or preheat oven to 400°F. In a bowl, combine oil, balsamic vinegar, oregano, salt, and pepper.

- Thread drumsticks onto skewers that have been soaked in water for 30 minutes. Balance skewers on the edges of a high-sided oven-safe rectangular pan, making sure the chicken does not touch the bottom of the dish.

- Brush drumsticks with sauce, and pour ½ cup water into bottom of pan.

- Place pan on barbecue grill or oven rack. Halfway through cooking, deglaze pan with a spatula and add remaining water. Turn skewers occasionally to ensure a golden brown skin, brushing with marinade each time.

- Serve with a green salad.

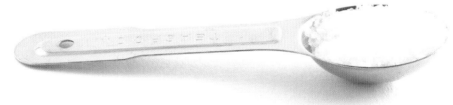

Chicken and Sage with a Balsamic Glaze

Honey, balsamic vinegar and spices compose a symphony of flavor delivered right to your table!

DIFFICULTY |

HEALTH BENEFITS | ♡ ♡ ♡ ♡

Prep time	10 minutes
Cook time	20 minutes

Ingredients

Serves 4

- 4 tbsp flour
- ¼ tsp salt
- ¼ tsp freshly ground black pepper
- 4 boneless chicken breasts
- 2 tbsp olive oil
- 3 cloves garlic, minced
- ½ tsp dried sage (or rosemary)
- 1 cup (250 ml) chicken stock
- 2 tbsp balsamic vinegar
- 2 tsp liquid honey
- 1 tbsp fresh parsley, chopped

Preparation

- In a sealable plastic bag, combine flour, salt and pepper. Add chicken breasts and shake well to coat. Reserve flour mixture.

- Heat half the oil in a large non-stick frying pan. Add chicken and cook for 12 minutes, turning once, or until chicken is no longer pink inside. Remove from pan and keep warm in a serving dish.

- Heat remaining oil, add garlic and sage, and cook over low heat for about 1 minute or until garlic has softened.

- Add remaining flour mixture and stir with a wooden spoon for 30 seconds. Add chicken stock, balsamic vinegar, and honey until sauce is thick enough to coat the back of a spoon.

- Put chicken pieces and any juices that may have accumulated on the resting dish back into frying pan. Coat with sauce and cook for about 1 minute or until chicken is fully glazed.

- Sprinkle with parsley right before serving.

Penne with Chicken and Peppers

Basil and sweet peppers brighten up this exquisitely creamy pasta dish garnished with freshly grated Parmesan.

DIFFICULTY |

HEALTH BENEFITS | ♡ ♡ ♡

Prep time	20 minutes
Cook time	30 minutes

Ingredients
Serves 4

- 1 tbsp oil
- 1 onion, finely chopped
- 2 cloves garlic, minced
- 1 cup (250 ml) mushrooms, sliced
- 1 cup (250 ml) peppers, sliced (⅓ red, ⅓ orange, ⅓ yellow)
- 2 chicken breasts, cubed
- ½ cup (125 ml) chicken stock
- 3 tbsp apple cider vinegar
- 1 ½ cups (375 ml) penne, cooked *al dente*
- 1 ½ cups (375 ml) hot milk
- ½ cup (125 ml) freshly grated Parmesan
- 1 tsp basil
- 4 tbsp fresh parsley

Preparation

- Heat oil in a large non-stick pan and sauté onion, garlic, mushrooms, and peppers.

- Add chicken and cook for 5 minutes over high heat.

- Remove chicken and vegetables from pan and set aside. Deglaze pan with chicken stock and vinegar.

- Transfer chicken and vegetables back to pan and add cooked penne, hot milk, salt, pepper, and cheese.

- Cook until sauce is smooth and creamy.

- Serve and top with basil and parsley.

Beer-Braised Rabbit with Prunes

Rabbit is stewed to tender succulence with sherry vinegar, beer, raisins, and thyme in this rustic dish that recalls the flavors of long ago.

DIFFICULTY |

HEALTH BENEFITS | ♡ ♡ ♡ ♡

Prep time	30 minutes
Cook time	1 hour

Ingredients
Serves 4

- 1 lb pitted prunes
- 2 ½ lbs rabbit, cut into pieces
- 1 tbsp butter
- 2 onions, chopped or 1 cup (250 ml) white or red pearl onions
- Salt and freshly ground pepper
- 1 tbsp brown sugar
- 3 cups (750 ml) beer
- 3 tbsp raisins
- 3 tbsp sherry vinegar
- 1 sprig thyme
- 1 bay leaf

Preparation

- To rehydrate prunes, place in a bowl with a bit of water and microwave for 1 minute, or cover prunes with boiling water and let sit until soft and tender.

- Cut rabbit into pieces and brown in butter in a large sauté pan.

- Remove rabbit from pan and set aside. Sauté onions until golden brown. Return rabbit to pan with salt, pepper, brown sugar, and beer (or water, if preferred).

- Add prunes, raisins, sherry vinegar, thyme, and bay leaf. Adjust seasoning to taste.

- Stew rabbit over low heat, until meat is tender and falls off the bone.

Prunes are extremely rich in fiber. Rabbit is low in calories and is a good source of protein and essential amino acids such as lysine, leucine, and arginine. It is also a source of vitamins B_3 and B_{12}, phosphorus, and selenium.

Zesty Citrus Duck Breast

This sophisticated main course will seduce even the most fervent foodies at the table, and is easier to prepare than most duck dishes. Perfect for any special occasion!

DIFFICULTY | 🎩 🎩 🎩 🎩

HEALTH BENEFITS | ♡ ♡

Prep time   30 minutes

Cook time   30 minutes

Ingredients
Serves 4

- 2 duck breasts
- 4 tbsp concentrated orange juice
- 4 tbsp sugar
- 4 tbsp red wine vinegar
- 1 cup (250 ml) prepared demi-glace (store-bought)
- 4 tbsp orange zest, blanched
- 1 tsp lime zest, blanched
- Salt and pepper to taste
- 2 tbsp Grand Marnier or orange liqueur
- 2 navel oranges, peeled and sectioned, pith and membranes removed
- 1 grapefruit, peeled and sectioned, pith and membranes removed

Preparation

- With a knife, score the fat of the duck breasts in a diamond pattern.

- Pan-sear duck breasts in a heavy skillet, flesh side down. Transfer to a baking sheet, fat side down, and finish cooking in a 350°F oven until medium-rare.

- Combine sugar and red wine vinegar, and deglaze skillet. Add demi-glace (prepared according to package directions) and blanched zests. Cook for a few minutes, adjust seasoning, and add Grand Marnier.

- Slice duck thinly. Spoon sauce over slices and garnish plate with citrus sections.

- Serve with roasted root vegetables (carrots, turnips, parsnips, beets, or potatoes).

Duck Breasts with Sherry Vinegar

Dress up this delicacy with a savory sauce that showcases the intensity and sweet finish of sherry vinegar.

DIFFICULTY |

HEALTH BENEFITS |

Prep time   10 minutes

Cook time   30 minutes

Ingredients

Serves 4

- 2 duck breasts
- 4 tbsp soy sauce
- 4 tbsp sherry vinegar
- 1 cup (250 ml) chicken stock

Preparation

- With a knife, score the skin of the duck breasts in a diamond pattern. Brush breasts with soy sauce.

- Place duck breasts fat side down in a hot non-stick pan and sear for a few minutes until golden brown.

- Remove breasts from pan, drain fat, and return to pan, flesh side down. Lower heat and cook about 5 minutes.

- Remove duck and finish cooking in oven at 350°F until medium-rare.

- Deglaze pan juices with vinegar and reduce for several minutes.

- Add chicken stock. Bring to a boil and cook over low heat until the sauce has reduced by half.

- Spoon sauce over duck and serve.

Duck is low in cholesterol, rich in nutrients, and an excellent source of phosphorus, iron, zinc, copper, selenium, and vitamins B_2, B_3, and B_5.

Veal & Beef

Veal Liver with Sherry Vinegar

Rich, sweet veal liver really stands out under a blanket of deliciously uncomplicated sherry vinegar sauce

DIFFICULTY |

HEALTH BENEFITS | ♡ ♡ ♡ ♡

Prep time   10 minutes
Cook time   15 minutes

Ingredients
Serves 4

- 1 packet store-bought demi-glace sauce mix
- 1 lb veal liver, sliced
- 2 tbsp butter
- 2 tbsp olive oil
- 4 tbsp sherry vinegar
- 2 tbsp parsley, finely chopped
- Salt and pepper

Preparation

- Prepare demi-glace according to package directions and set aside.

- In a non-stick pan, cook liver in oil and butter. Remove from pan and keep warm.

- Deglaze pan with vinegar and reduce by half. Add parsley, salt, and pepper. Add demi-glace and veal to pan; cook for 1 or 2 minutes. Serve immediately.

Veal liver is an excellent source of vitamin A, vitamin B12, and iron. Combine vinegar and veal for a meal that's not only healthy, but delicious, too!

Mexican Braised Beef

A comforting autumn meal packed with nourishing vegetables.

DIFFICULTY |

HEALTH BENEFITS |

Prep time   20 minutes

Cook time   2 hours

Preparation

- In a Dutch oven, brown beef in olive oil. Remove and set aside.

- In Dutch oven, sauté celery, peppers, garlic, and onion, then add tomatoes, vegetable juice, brown sugar, vinegar, Tabasco sauce, salt, and pepper. Add beef, and cook in the oven at 350°F (180°C) for 2 hours until meat is tender.

- One hour into cooking, add quartered potatoes that have been washed and peeled.

Ingredients

Serves 4

- 2 lbs beef, cubed
- Olive oil
- 2 celery stalks, cut into large pieces
- 1 red and 1 orange pepper, cut into large pieces
- 2 cloves garlic, minced
- 1 large red onion, cut into large pieces
- 1 large can diced tomatoes
- 2 cups (500 ml) store-bought vegetable juice
- 3 tbsp brown sugar
- 5 tbsp apple cider vinegar
- A few drops Tabasco sauce
- Salt and pepper
- A few potatoes

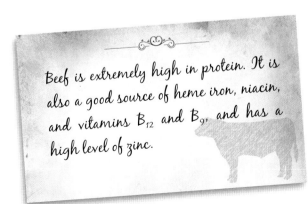

Beef is extremely high in protein. It is also a good source of heme iron, niacin, and vitamins B_{12} and B_9, and has a high level of zinc.

Beef with Chanterelles and Raspberry Vinegar

Fruity chanterelle mushrooms create a delectable duet with raspberry vinegar – a true gourmet delight!

| Prep time | 10 minutes |
| Cook time | 20 minutes |

DIFFICULTY |

HEALTH BENEFITS | ♡ ♡ ♥

Ingredients
Serves 4

- 1 lb beef tenderloin or sirloin cut into strips
- Salt and freshly ground pepper
- 2 tbsp butter
- 4 tsp raspberry vinegar
- ½ cup (125 ml) beef consommé
- ½ cup (125 ml) 35% cream
- 3 tbsp butter
- 1 cup (250 ml) chanterelle mushrooms

Preparation

- Season beef strips with salt and pepper. Melt butter in a non-stick frying pan over high heat and add beef strips. Let beef cook for 20 or 30 seconds without stirring to allow them to brown. Drain and set aside.

- Reduce heat, deglaze with raspberry vinegar, add consommé and cream, and reduce sauce by ⅓. Season.

- Before serving beef, gently sauté chanterelles in remaining butter over low heat to prevent them from losing their tenderness. Season with salt and pepper.

- Spoon sauce over beef and garnish with mushrooms.

Veal Cutlets with Balsamic and Portobellos

Portobello mushrooms and balsamic vinegar have been long-time companions.
Just add veal and voila! An inseparable trio is formed!

DIFFICULTY |

HEALTH BENEFITS |

Prep time	15 minutes
Cook time	12 minutes

Ingredients
Serves 4

- 3 portobello mushrooms
- 1 tbsp butter
- 1 tbsp olive oil
- 1 tbsp balsamic vinegar
- 8 veal cutlets
- 2 tbsp flour
- 4 sprigs fresh oregano

Preparation

- Clean and slice mushrooms.

- Heat half of the butter and half of the oil in a non-stick pan over high heat and cook mushrooms until golden. Deglaze with balsamic vinegar and set aside.

- Dredge each cutlet in flour and brown in remaining butter and oil, approximately 2 minutes per side.

- For each serving, start by layering mushrooms on bottom, then alternate between layers of veal cutlets and mushrooms. Decorate each stack with a sprig of oregano and serve with basmati rice and steamed broccoli.

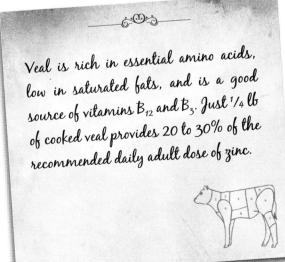

Veal is rich in essential amino acids, low in saturated fats, and is a good source of vitamins B_{12} and B_3. Just ¼ lb of cooked veal provides 20 to 30% of the recommended daily adult dose of zinc.

Barbecued Balsamic-Marsala Veal Medallions

A true classic, cooked on the barbecue.

DIFFICULTY |

HEALTH BENEFITS | ♡ ♡ ♡

Prep time   25 minutes

Cook time   12 minutes

Ingredients

Serves 4

- 1 ½ lbs veal medallions
- 2 tbsp olive oil
- 2 tsp balsamic vinegar
- 1 shallot, minced
- 2 tbsp butter
- ¼ cup (60 ml) Marsala wine
- ¾ cup (180 ml) store-bought veal stock
- 4 asparagus spears, cut diagonally into thirds
- 2 artichoke hearts, patted dry and quartered
- 4 sundried tomatoes, julienned
- 2 tbsp olive oil

Preparation

- Preheat barbecue

- Coat veal medallions in oil and vinegar before cooking. Barbecue for 2 minutes on each side; remove from grill and keep warm.

- In a skillet, sauté onions in butter. Deglaze with Marsala, add veal stock, and reduce sauce until thick. Season and set aside.

- Add remaining 2 tablespoons olive oil to skillet and sauté asparagus, artichokes, and sundried tomatoes.

- Arrange veal on four warmed plates and serve with sauce and sautéed asparagus, artichokes, and sundried tomatoes.

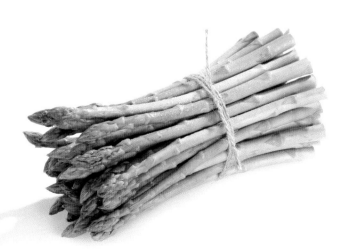

Veal Liver with Balsamic and Pine Nuts

*Pine nuts give a deep, nutty flavor that complements
the simple balsamic sauce and sweet veal liver.*

DIFFICULTY |

HEALTH BENEFITS | ♡ ♡ ♡ ♡

| Prep time | 5 minutes |
| Cook time | 10 minutes |

Ingredients
Serves 4

- 2 large onions, thinly sliced
- 2 tbsp olive oil
- ½ cup (125 ml) pine nuts
- 1 lb veal liver cut into thin slices
- ½ cup flour
- 2 tbsp butter
- Salt and pepper
- 4 tbsp balsamic or red wine vinegar

Preparation

- In a non-stick pan, gently cook onions in oil until lightly golden. Add pine nuts and cook for 1 or 2 minutes more.

- Transfer to a serving plate and keep warm. Dredge liver in flour. In the same pan, brown butter and then add veal and sauté for 1 to 2 minutes on each side. Add salt and pepper.

- As soon as it has finished cooking, place cooked veal on bed of onions. Remove cooking fat from pan, deglaze with vinegar, and pour over liver.

- Serve with potatoes and green vegetables.

Veal Liver with Raspberry Vinegar

Fresh raspberries and a splash of raspberry vinegar balance out the richness of the liver in this quick bistro-inspired dish.

DIFFICULTY |

HEALTH BENEFITS | ♡ ♡ ♡ ♡

Prep time   5 minutes
Cook time   15 minutes

Ingredients
Serves 2

- 1 tsp butter
- 2 slices veal liver
- 2 tbsp raspberry vinegar
- 1 tbsp water
- 1 tsp honey
- Salt and freshly ground pepper
- 1 pint raspberries
- Fresh parsley, chopped

Preparation

- Brown butter in a non-stick pan and cook unsalted liver for 8 to 10 minutes over medium heat according to thickness and desired doneness, turning halfway through cooking. Veal is best served slightly pink.

- Arrange liver in a serving dish and cover with foil. Keep warm in a 140°F oven.

- Discard fat. Pour raspberry vinegar and water into pan and deglaze by scraping up drippings with a wooden spoon.

- Add honey and stir for about 1 minute, then add a bit of salt and pepper. Pour in any juices released by reserved veal.

- Remove pan from heat and add raspberries. Stir gently to keep raspberries whole.

- Pour sauce over warm liver, sprinkle with fresh chopped parsley, and serve with mashed potatoes and a tomato Parmesan gratin.

Vegetarian & Side Dishes

Easy Dinnertime Soup

*This soup is quick to make, packed with healthy ingredients,
and ultra-comforting on a cold winter night.*

DIFFICULTY |

HEALTH BENEFITS | ♡ ♡ ♡ ♡

Prep time	20 minutes
Cook time	45 minutes

Preparation

- Heat olive oil in a large pot. Add onions and garlic and cook until soft.

- Add potatoes, carrots, and celery. Continue cooking, stirring occasionally. Add tomatoes and cook for 3 minutes.

- Pour in chicken or vegetable stock and add bay leaf, thyme, salt, and pepper.

- Bring soup to a boil and let simmer over low heat for 30 minutes. Add chickpeas, kidney beans, and pasta, and cook for another 15 minutes until pasta is *al dente*.

- Before serving, remove bay leaf. Keep soup in the refrigerator for up to a week.

Ingredients
Serves 8

- 3 tbsp olive oil

- 2 onions, finely chopped

- 1 clove garlic, minced

- 2 medium potatoes, peeled and diced

- 4 carrots, thinly sliced into rounds

- 4 celery stalks, thinly sliced

- 1 can diced tomatoes

- 10 cups chicken or vegetable stock

- 1 bay leaf

- ½ tsp dried thyme

- 1 tsp salt

- ½ tsp pepper

- ¼ cup (60 ml) canned chickpeas, drained

- ½ cup (125 ml) red kidney beans

- ½ cup (125 ml) macaroni or shell pasta

Zesty Gazpacho

Relish all the flavors of summer with a smooth, cool, refreshing soup that will tickle your taste buds with a kick of cayenne.

Prep time	20 minutes
Wait time	2 hours
Refrigeration time	4 hours

DIFFICULTY |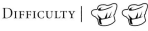

HEALTH BENEFITS | ♡ ♡ ♡ ♡ ♡

Ingredients
Serves 6

- 1 cucumber
- 1 ½ lbs fresh tomatoes
- 1 red pepper
- 1 green pepper
- 1 onion
- 2 to 4 cloves garlic
- ⅓ cup (80 ml) olive oil
- 1 cup bread (about ½ baguette), torn into pieces
- 3 tbsp sherry vinegar
- ⁴⁄₅ cup (200 ml) water
- Cayenne pepper

For garnish

- 2 tomatoes
- 1 cucumber
- ½ pepper
- Croutons
- 4 tbsp olive oil

Preparation

- Peel cucumber, remove seeds, and cut into pieces. Score each tomato with an "X" and scald by dropping into boiling water for 30 seconds, then immersing in cold water. Peel, remove seeds, and cut into quarters. Remove seeds from peppers, then dice. Peel onion and garlic and roughly chop. Place all vegetables in a bowl and add salt and olive oil. Let sit at room temperature for 2 hours.

- In a bowl, pour vinegar and water over bread pieces and let marinate.

- Pour vegetables and any vegetable juices into a mixing bowl. Add soaked bread and puree the mixture, seasoning with salt as desired. Add pepper and a pinch of cayenne. Chill gazpacho in the refrigerator for at least 4 hours.

- To prepare garnish, dice tomatoes, cucumber, and pepper. Place in small side dishes. Serve chilled gazpacho in cups or bowls with vegetable mixture and croutons on the side.

Sautéed Green Beans

This bright, crunchy side dish is the perfect accompaniment to any meal.

DIFFICULTY |

HEALTH BENEFITS | ♡ ♡ ♡ ♡ ♡

Prep time   15 minutes

Cook time   5 minutes

Ingredients

- 2 lbs green beans, sliced and cooked
- 4 tbsp olive oil
- 3 cloves garlic, minced
- 2 tbsp apple cider vinegar
- ½ tsp fresh thyme
- ½ tsp sea salt

Preparation

- Sauté cooked green beans in olive oil..
- Add garlic and cook for 1 to 2 minutes.
- Add vinegar and season with remaining ingredients.
- Serve hot as a side dish.

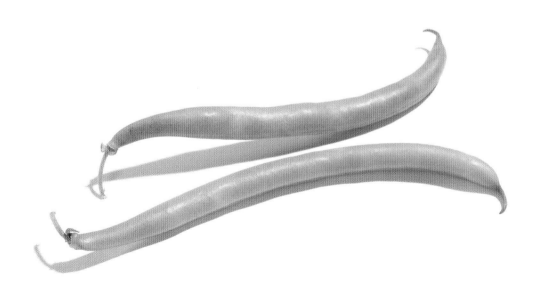

Ricotta-Stuffed Potatoes Au Gratin

A creamy, cheesy alternative to traditional baked potatoes!

DIFFICULTY |

HEALTH BENEFITS | ♡ ♡

Prep time   15 minutes
Cook time   35 minutes

Ingredients
Serves 4

- 4 quality potatoes
- 2 cloves garlic
- 12 fresh basil leaves
- A few stalks of fresh chives
- Fresh parsley
- ½ cup (125 ml) ricotta cheese
- 1 tbsp balsamic vinegar
- Salt and freshly ground pepper
- Cheddar cheese for gratin
- Arugula

Preparation

- Wash and scrub potatoes with a brush under running water.

- Preheat oven to 400°F, placing rack in the middle of the oven. Bake potatoes for about 35 minutes or until they are soft and tender.

- In a food processor, combine garlic, basil, chives, and fresh parsley. Add ricotta, balsamic vinegar, pepper, and a small amount of salt.

- Cut baked potatoes lengthwise and gently scoop out a small amount of flesh. Stuff with ricotta mixture and top with cheddar cheese.

- Broil for a few minutes and serve on a bed of arugula.

Marinated Button Mushrooms

Try this tasty recipe with cremini or oyster mushrooms!

DIFFICULTY |
HEALTH BENEFITS | ♡ ♡ ♡ ♡

Prep time	20 minutes
Cook time	2 minutes
Marinating time	12 hours

Mushrooms contain essential nutrients including selenium, vitamins B_1, B_2, B_3, and B_5, potassium, copper (up to 0.6 mg), protein, iron, vitamin D, and fiber.

Ingredients
Serves 4

- ¾ lb button mushrooms
- 3 tbsp wine vinegar
- 2 tbsp olive oil
- 1 tbsp lemon juice
- ⅖ cup (100 ml) tomato puree
- 1 small bay leaf
- Pinch of brown sugar
- 1 tsp coriander seeds
- Salt and pepper
- Chopped parsley or cilantro to garnish

Preparation

- Remove dirty stem bottoms from mushrooms. If mushrooms are large, cut into quarters. Put into a bowl.

- In a pot, combine vinegar, olive oil, lemon juice, tomato puree, bay leaf, brown sugar, coriander seeds, salt, and pepper, and bring to a boil, stirring often. Cook for 2 minutes.

- Pour boiling mixture over mushrooms and marinate overnight in the refrigerator. The mushrooms will release their flavor, creating a deliciously fragrant sauce.

- Serve fresh, garnished with chopped parsley or cilantro.

Pasta with Fennel and Swiss Chard

The delicate bitterness of Swiss chard pairs perfectly
with the pleasant sweetness of fennel and balsamic vinegar.

DIFFICULTY |

HEALTH BENEFITS | ♡ ♡ ♡ ♡ ♡

Prep time   15 minutes
Cook time   20 minutes

Ingredients

Serves 4

- ¼ cup (60 ml) olive oil
- 1 onion, finely chopped
- 1 bulb fennel, stalks removed and thinly sliced
- 2 cloves garlic, minced
- ¾ cup (180 ml) water
- 4 tbsp balsamic vinegar
- Salt and pepper
- Pinch of hot pepper flakes
- 8 cups pasta
- 1 lb swiss chard leaves, roughly chopped
- ½ cup (125 ml) Parmesan cheese

Preparation

- Heat oil in a large non-stick frying pan and cook onion for about 5 minutes. Add fennel and garlic and fry until it colors, about 10 minutes.

- Deglaze pan with water and vinegar, cover half of pan with lid and let the liquid evaporate completely over medium-high heat. Add salt, pepper, and hot pepper flakes.

- While the liquid is reducing, bring 1 gallon of salted water to a boil in a large pot. Cook pasta to desired doneness. Add Swiss chard to boiling water 2 minutes before draining pasta.

- Drain pasta and chard, reserving 1 cup (250 ml) pasta water. Add to fennel mixture and add Parmesan and a bit of olive oil. If it seems too dry, add some reserved pasta water.

- Toss well and serve in heated bowls. Garnish with raw fennel slices, Parmesan, and freshly ground pepper.

Roasted Pear and Roquefort Tarts

The sweetness of pears marries with the piquant creaminess of Roquefort to create an indulgent appetizer or sweet and savory dessert.

DIFFICULTY |

HEALTH BENEFITS | ♡ ♡ ♡ ♡

Prep time	15 minutes
Cook time	15 minutes

Preparation

- Line 4 tart dishes with puff pastry.

- Peel pears, cut in half, remove cores and seeds, and slice. Lightly crush walnut halves. Slice Roquefort and place at the bottom of each tart.

- Layer nuts over cheese, and spread pears evenly on top of nuts. Brush with melted butter and bake for about 12 minutes in a 350°F oven.

- In a small saucepan, bring 6 tbsp Banyuls vinegar to a boil. Remove from heat, add remaining 2 tbsp vinegar, and transfer to a bowl. Add salt and pepper, and then add oil in a steady stream to create an emulsion.

- Place tarts on separate serving dishes and spoon 1 tsp vinaigrette over each tart.

Ingredients

Serves 4

- ½ lb store-bought puff pastry
- 2 pears
- 1 or 2 tbsp walnuts
- ½ cup (125 ml) Roquefort or another blue cheese
- 2 tbsp melted butter
- 8 tbsp Banyuls or balsamic vinegar
- Salt and freshly ground pepper
- 3 tbsp peanut oil

Black Bean Salsa

Serve this ever-so-slightly spicy salsa as a side with chips or as a light lunch salad.

DIFFICULTY |

HEALTH BENEFITS | ♡ ♡ ♡ ♡

| Prep time | 15 minutes |
| Wait time e | 1 hour |

Preparation

- In a glass bowl, combine black beans, tomatoes, onions, garlic, cilantro, peppers, jalapeños, vinegar, and sugar. Toss well. Add salt and pepper to taste.

- Let sit for 1 hour before serving, stirring occasionally.

Ingredients
Serves 4

- 1 can black beans
- 2 tomatoes, seeded and diced
- 2 green onions, chopped
- 2 tablespoons white onion, chopped
- 1 clove garlic, minced
- ¾ cup (180 ml) fresh cilantro, chopped
- 2 tbsp red pepper, chopped
- 2 tbsp green pepper, chopped
- 2 tbsp jalapeños pepper, chopped
- 1 tbsp balsamic vinegar
- 1 tbsp sugar
- Salt and freshly ground pepper

Salads & Vinaigrettes

Cabbage Slaw with Fresh Herbs

A classic salad gets a fresh new twist with savory herbs and an apple cider vinegar dressing.

DIFFICULTY |

HEALTH BENEFITS | ♡ ♡ ♡ ♡

Prep time   10 minutes

Wait time   A few hours

Ingredients

Serves 4

- 2 cups (500 ml) cabbage, grated
- 2 tbsp mayonnaise
- 4 tbsp sugar
- 2 tbsp fresh chives, chopped
- 2 tbsp apple cider vinegar
- 2 tbsp milk
- Onion salt to taste
- Salt and freshly ground pepper to taste

Preparation

- Combine ingredients and chill in the refrigerator for a few hours.

Variation

- Combine 5 cups grated cabbage, ¼ cup (60 ml) grated carrots, ¼ cup (60 ml) finely chopped onions, 2 tbsp sugar, a pinch of dry mustard, ½ cup (125 ml) vegetable oil, salt, and pepper.

Red-Skinned Potato Salad

Here's a simple creamy yet tangy potato salad, perfect for barbecues or potlucks!

DIFFICULTY |

HEALTH BENEFITS | ♡ ♡ ♡

Prep time	20 minutes
Cook time	20 minutes

Preparation

- Boil unpeeled potatoes. Let cool; peel and cut into cubes.

- In a bowl, combine green onions, yogurt, mayonnaise, vinegar, mustard, salt, and curry powder.

- Pour dressing over potatoes, add pepper and parsley, and gently toss to coat.

Ingredients

- 2 lbs red-skinned potatoes
- 4 green onions, chopped
- ⅓ cup (80 ml) plain yogurt
- ⅓ cup (80 ml) mayonnaise
- 2 tsp apple cider vinegar
- 1 tsp Dijon mustard
- 1 tsp salt
- 1 tsp curry powder
- Freshly ground pepper
- 2 tbsp fresh parsley, chopped

Simple Caesar Salad

The secret to the perfect classic Caesar salad is using only the freshest, highest-quality ingredients and real Parmesan cheese.

DIFFICULTY |

HEALTH BENEFITS | ♡ ♡ ♡

Prep time	10 minutes
Wait time	1 hour
Cook time	10 minutes

Ingredients

- 2 cloves garlic
- 3 tbsp wine vinegar
- 1 tbsp Dijon mustard
- 1 egg
- ½ cup (125 ml) canola oil
- 1 head romaine lettuce
- 6 slices bacon
- ½ cup (125 ml) grated Parmesan cheese
- Croutons

Preparation

- In a blender, combine the first five ingredients, adding them one by one in the order provided. Chill in refrigerator for at least 1 hour.

- Wash romaine lettuce and dry using a salad spinner.

- While waiting for dressing, cook and drain 6 slices bacon.

- Add dressing, bacon broken up into bits, and croutons.

- Toss well and top with Parmesan cheese.

Chicken Salad with Curry Vinaigrette

Curry and yogurt add an unexpected richness to this delectably healthy salad packed with protein and fresh veggies.

DIFFICULTY |

HEALTH BENEFITS | ♡ ♡ ♡ ♡

Prep time   20 minutes

Cook time   10 minutes

Ingredients

- 1 cup (250 ml) plain yogurt
- ¼ cup (60 ml) 10% cream
- 2 tbsp mango chutney
- 2 tbsp green onions, finely chopped
- 1 tsp curry powder
- 2 tbsp apple cider vinegar
- 2 tbsp shallots, minced
- 2 chicken breasts
- Romaine lettuce, shredded
- 1 cup (250 ml) cherry tomatoes
- 1 English cucumber
- 1 large carrot, julienned
- Salt and freshly ground pepper

Preparation

- Preheat barbecue.

- In a bowl, combine yogurt, cream, chutney, onions, curry powder, vinegar, and shallot. Brush chicken breasts with 2 tbsp of the vinaigrette and place on hot grill.

- With the barbecue lid down, cook over medium heat for 10 minutes or until chicken is no longer pink inside, turning halfway through. Remove from grill and slice into strips.

- In a large salad bowl, combine chicken, lettuce, tomatoes, cucumber, and carrots. Toss lightly with curry vinaigrette. Salt and pepper to taste.

Pear and Spinach Salad

*Sweet pears and a dash of zippy red wine vinegar transform
a simple salad into a heavenly taste experience.*

DIFFICULTY |

HEALTH BENEFITS | ♡ ♡ ♡ ♡

Prep time   10 minutes

Cook time   10 minutes

Try this salad with a blue cheese dressing!

See page 193

Preparation

- In a medium bowl, combine sour cream, mayonnaise, Worcestershire sauce, vinegar, salt, pepper, and blue cheese. Set aside.

- Cook and drain bacon.

- To serve, put spinach, pear slices, bacon, and walnuts in a salad bowl and toss lightly.

- Divide salad into 6 equal portions, plate, and serve dressing on the side.

Ingredients

Serves 6

- ⅓ cup (80 ml) sour cream

- ½ cup (125 ml) mayonnaise

- ½ tsp Worcestershire sauce

- 1 tbsp red wine vinegar

- Salt and pepper

- ¼ cup blue cheese, crumbled

- 6 slices bacon

- 6 cups baby spinach

- 3 pears, peeled, cored, thinly sliced, and dipped in cider vinegar

- 1 cup (250 ml) walnuts

Italian Salad

A simple salad dressed up with an aromatic herb and cider vinegar...

DIFFICULTY |

HEALTH BENEFITS | ♡ ♡ ♡ ♡ ♡

Prep time   10 minutes

Preparation

- In a food processor or with a whisk, blend apple cider vinegar, garlic, oregano, thyme, basil, cayenne pepper, and sugar. Gradually blend in the oil.

- In a large bowl, combine spinach, onion, and vinaigrette. Salt and pepper to taste.

- Serve.

Ingredients

- ¼ cup (60 ml) apple cider vinegar
- 1 clove garlic, minced
- ½ tsp dried oregano
- ½ tsp dried thyme
- ½ tsp dried basil
- ½ tsp cayenne pepper
- Pinch of sugar
- ⅓ cup extra virgin olive oil
- 1 ½ lbs fresh spinach, washed with stems removed
- 1 medium red onion, finely chopped
- Salt and freshly ground pepper

Celeriac Salad

The root of the celery plant has a mild, delicate flavor that is enhanced with cider vinegar and a generous splash of tart lemon juice.

DIFFICULTY |

HEALTH BENEFITS | ♡ ♡ ♡ ♡

Prep time   15 minutes

Ingredients
Serves 4 to 6

- 1 celeriac
- Juice of 1 lemon
- 2 endives
- ½ cup (125 ml) fresh mushrooms
- 1 apple
- ½ cup (125 ml) mayonnaise
- 1 tbsp apple cider vinegar
- 1 pinch paprika
- Salt and freshly ground pepper
- 1 tbsp almonds, finely chopped

Preparation

- Peel and grate celeriac. Mix with lemon juice to keep it from turning brown.
- Cut endives into medium-sized pieces.
- Remove stems from mushrooms and cut into thin slices.
- Peel apple and cut into thin strips.
- Combine chopped ingredients and add mayonnaise, vinegar, paprika, salt, and pepper.
- Sprinkle with almonds right before serving.

Two-Bean Salad with Feta

A bright, appetizing, nutrient-packed salad that can be made year-round as a side dish or easy main course. .

Difficulty |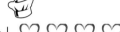

Health Benefits | ♡ ♡ ♡ ♡

Ingredients
Serves 4 to 6

- 1 can red kidney beans, drained and rinsed
- 1 can chickpeas, drained and rinsed
- 3 tomatoes, diced
- 2 cups (500 ml) fresh parsley, roughly chopped
- ½ green or red pepper, chopped
- ½ cup (125 ml) feta cheese, cut into small cubes
- ⅓ cup (80 ml) red onion, chopped

Preparation

- Combine all ingredients. Add vinaigrette and toss to coat.

Lemon Dijon Vinaigrette

A bean salad's perfect companion!

Difficulty |

Health Benefits | ♡ ♡ ♡ ♡

Ingredients

- 2 tbsp canola oil
- 1 tbsp lemon juice
- ½ tbsp apple cider vinegar
- ½ tbsp Dijon mustard
- Salt and freshly ground pepper to taste

Preparation

- Combine ingredients and pour over salad.

Beet and Endive Salad

A few classic ingredients added to leafy greens create
an elegant balance of colors, flavors, and aromas.

Difficulty |

Health Benefits | ♡ ♡ ♡ ♡ ♡

Prep time   15 minutes

Cook time   12 minutes

Ingredients

- 2 small beets
- 3 endives
- 2 cups (500 ml) watercress
- 1 tsp Dijon mustard
- 1 tbsp apple cider vinegar
- 1 pinch sugar
- Salt and freshly ground pepper
- 1 shallot, minced
- ¼ cup (60 ml) olive oil

Preparation

- Cook beets in microwave in a small amount of water for about 12 minutes. Let cool. Peel and slice.

- Combine endive leaves, beets, and watercress in a salad bowl.

- In another bowl, prepare vinaigrette by combining mustard, vinegar, sugar, salt, pepper, and shallot, and then slowly add oil in a steady stream.

- Dress salad.

Mango-Cucumber Salad

Summary calls for a refreshing salad of sweet mangoes and cool cucumbers!

DIFFICULTY |

HEALTH BENEFITS | ♡ ♡ ♡ ♡

Prep time   10 minutes

Preparation

- Peel and slice cucumber. Set aside.
- Peel and thinly slice mango. Place slices in center of serving plate.
- Place cucumber slices around mango. Garnish with chives.
- Prepare a simple vinaigrette with grape seed oil and balsamic vinegar. Dress salad.

Ingredients
Serves 1

- ½ cucumber
- ½ mango
- A few stalks of chives
- Balsamic vinegar
- Grape seed oil

Creamy Yogurt Pasta Salad

Jazz up the weeknight dinner routine with this deceptively rich-tasting low-fat pasta salad.

DIFFICULTY |

HEALTH BENEFITS | ♡ ♡ ♡

Prep time　　　　30 minutes

Ingredients

Serves 4 to 6

- 1 tsp Dijon mustard
- 3 tbsp apple cider vinegar
- Salt and freshly ground pepper
- ½ cup (125 ml) plain yogurt
- ½ cup (125 ml) light mayonnaise
- 6 tbsp olive oil
- 2 tbsp each of parsley and basil, chopped
- 3 cups (750 ml) farfalle, cooked
- 1 English cucumber, diced
- 1 red pepper, diced
- 1 green pepper, diced
- 2 green onions, finely chopped

Preparation

- Combine mustard, vinegar, salt, pepper, yogurt, and mayonnaise. Add oil by pouring in a steady stream, stirring constantly. Add fresh herbs.

- In a large salad bowl, combine pasta, cucumber, peppers, and green onions. Add vinaigrette and toss to coat.

Pineapple Chicken Salad

Sweet pineapple complements tender chicken slices, and chopped nuts provide toothsome crunch.

DIFFICULTY |

HEALTH BENEFITS | ♡ ♡ ♡ ♡

Prep time — 15 minutes

Ingredients

- 2 chicken breasts, cooked and cut into strips
- 1 pineapple, cubed
- 1 celery stalk, chopped on the diagonal
- 2 tbsp nuts, chopped
- ½ cup (125 ml) mayonnaise
- 2 tsp curry powder
- 1 tsp apple cider vinegar
- 1 head Boston lettuce
- ½ tsp fresh chives, chopped

Preparation

- In a large bowl, combine chicken, pineapple, celery, and nuts.
- In another bowl, combine mayonnaise, curry powder, and vinegar.
- Add dressing to chicken mixture and toss to coat.
- Arrange lettuce leaves on a plate and top with salad. Garnish with chives.

Country Sausage Salad

This protein-rich salad provides energy throughout the day while still packing a flavor punch!.

DIFFICULTY |

HEALTH BENEFITS | ♡ ♡ ♡

Prep time   15 minutes

Ingredients
Serves 4

- 1 head romaine lettuce
- ¼ cup (60 ml) white cabbage, grated
- ¼ cup (60 ml) red cabbage, grated
- 2 carrots, grated
- ⅓ lb kielbasa, cubed
- ½ tsp chervil
- 5 tbsp sunflower oil
- 2 tbsp apple cider vinegar
- 1 tbsp Dijon mustard
- Salt and freshly ground pepper

Preparation

- Arrange lettuce on serving plates.
- Combine cabbage and carrots and spread over lettuce. Top with sausage and chervil.
- Mix oil, vinegar, and mustard. Salt and pepper to taste.
- Pour vinaigrette over salad and serve.

Moroccan Salad

A salad inspired by the vibrant flavors of North Africa — tangy lemon, salty olives, and fresh parsley.

DIFFICULTY |

HEALTH BENEFITS | ♡ ♡ ♡ ♡ ♡

Prep time   15 minutes

Ingredients
Serves 4

- 2 lemons
- 1 small red onion, thinly sliced
- 16 green olives, pits removed
- 3 tbsp parsley, chopped
- 1 pinch cumin
- 2 tsp apple cider vinegar
- Salt
- 4 tbsp olive oil

Preparation

- Soak lemons in cold, lightly salted water for 30 minutes. Remove lemons, peel, and cut in half. Squeeze and zest lemons, placing in separate bowls.

- Chop lemon zest and put in a salad bowl. Add onion, olives, parsley, paprika, cumin, and vinegar. Salt to taste and mix well.

- Add olive oil and lemon juice. Toss and serve immediately.

Tuna Avocado Salad

The combination of tuna and avocado is absolutely delicious — and nutritious!

DIFFICULTY |

HEALTH BENEFITS | ♡ ♡ ♡

Prep time   30 minutes

Preparation

- Pour juice of ½ lemon over diced avocados and set aside.

- In a bowl, toss vegetables and juice of another ½ lemon.

- Prepare vinaigrette with oil, remaining lemon juice, vinegar, and egg yolk.

- Whisk together, season with salt and pepper, and add to vegetables.

- Add avocados, drained tuna, grated cheese, and nuts. Serve immediately.

Ingredients

Serves 4

- Juice of 2 lemons

- 2 avocados, diced

- 1 small cauliflower, broken into florets and blanched for 2 minutes in boiling water

- ½ cup (125 ml) mushrooms, chopped

- 1 celery stalk, chopped

- 6 tbsp olive oil

- 2 tbsp apple cider vinegar

- 1 egg yolk

- 1 can flaked tuna, drained

- ¼ cup (60 ml) Gruyere cheese, grated

- 12 walnuts, chopped

- Salt and freshly ground pepper pepper

Basic Vinaigrette

DIFFICULTY |

HEALTH BENEFITS | ♡ ♡ ♡ ♡ ♡

Preparation

- In a bowl, combine mustard, garlic, salt, pepper, and vinegar. Pour in oil in a steady stream, whisking to form a smooth emulsion.

- Vinaigrette will keep for 1 month in the refrigerator.

Ingredients

- 1 tsp Dijon mustard
- 1 clove garlic, crushed
- Salt and freshly ground pepper
- ⅓ cup (80 ml) apple cider vinegar
- ⅔ cup (160 ml) vegetable oil

Blue Cheese Dressing

DIFFICULTY |

HEALTH BENEFITS | ♡

Ingredients

- ⅔ cup (160 ml) blue cheese, crumbled
- ½ cup (125 ml) sour cream
- 2 tsp Dijon mustard or horseradish
- 1 small clove garlic, crushed
- 1 tbsp cider vinegar
- ½ tsp pepper
- 1 pinch salt
- ⅓ cup (80 ml) canola oil

Preparation

- Combine blue cheese, sour cream, mustard, garlic, vinegar, pepper, and salt. Pour in oil in a steady stream, whisking to form a smooth emulsion.

- Use as a dressing for arugula, watercress, endive, escarole, leaf lettuce, crisp romaine lettuce, or even a chunk of iceberg lettuce. It can also be used as a dip for raw vegetables.

- For a thinner, lighter dressing, add buttermilk or milk until dressing is the desired consistency.

Honey-Mustard Vinaigrette

Difficulty |

Health Benefits | ♡ ♡ ♡

Preparation

- Combine all ingredients except oil. Pour in oil in a steady stream, whisking to form a smooth emulsion.

- Use as a dressing for red leaf lettuce, arugula, diced cucumbers, or sliced meats.

Ingredients

- 1 large clove garlic, minced
- 1 tbsp honey
- 1 tbsp mustard
- 2 tbsp lemon juice
- 5 tbsp extra virgin olive oil

Grapefruit Vinaigrette

Difficulty |

Health Benefits | ♡ ♡ ♡ ♡

Preparation

- Combine all ingredients.
- Use as a dressing for arugula, avocado, or your favorite salad.

Ingredients

- 3 tbsp grapefruit juice
- 4 tbsp olive oil
- 1 tbsp apple cider vinegar
- 1 tsp fresh herbs, chopped
- 1 tsp liquid honey
- Salt and freshly ground pepper

Quick Ketchup

DIFFICULTY |

HEALTH BENEFITS | ♡ ♡ ♡

Ingredients

- 1 small can tomato paste
- 4 tbsp brown sugar
- 4 tbsp water
- 2 tbsp apple cider vinegar
- ¼ tsp dry mustard
- 1 pinch ground cloves

Preparation

- Combine all ingredients in a glass bowl, mixing well. Keep in refrigerator for up to 1 month.

Variation

- Instead of canned tomato paste, boil 4 tomatoes for 30 seconds (score each with an "X" beforehand), and then peel.

- Blend in food processor to create a homemade puree.

Homemade Vinegars

Making flavored and perfumed vinegars at home is becoming increasingly popular – and it couldn't be easier! Adding flavors and aromatics to vinegars opens up a world of healthy possibilities and unique taste experiences.

Chive Vinegar

Chive vinegar pairs wonderfully with white fish, rice, risotto, or even pasta salad.

Prep time   30 minutes

Cook time   15 minutes

Steep time   2 weeks

Ingredients

- *Fines herbes* (whole unbloomed chives or a tarragon branch)
- 1 cup (250 ml) apple cider vinegar
- 1 bottle that can be sterilized in boiling water.

Preparation

- Wash *fines herbes* and dry with paper towel.
- For chives with seed pods, pierce pods to release air. If air is not released, chives will float at the surface of the vinegar.
- Boil vinegar.
- Slide *fines herbes* into a pretty bottle that has been sterilized. Pour hot vinegar into bottle over chives.
- Seal bottle tightly and let steep upside down for at least two weeks.

Adding garlic to homemade vinegars is not recommended, as it might turn rancid. If garlic is used, store vinegar in the refrigerator.

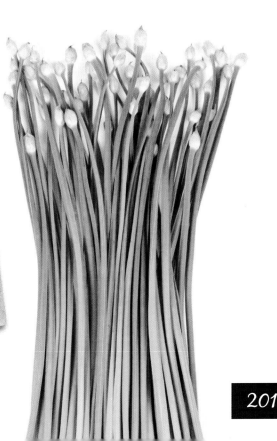

Spiced Vinegar

Add this vinegar to vinaigrettes, sauces, or oysters with delicately perfumed shallots.

Prep time   30 minutes

Cook time   10 minutes

Steep time   10 to 15 days

Ingredients

- 2 cinnamon sticks
- 2 mace flowers
- 1 tbsp whole cloves
- 1 tbsp black peppercorns
- 1 tbsp allspice
- 2 bay leaves
- 4 dried chili peppers
- 4 cups white or red wine vinegar

Preparation

- In a pot, combine spices, crumbled bay leaves, peppers, and vinegar.

- Heat almost to a boil and remove from heat. Do not allow mixture to boil.

- Let cool and pour into a clean, dry bottle. Seal tightly.

- Store in a cool, dry place for 10 to 15 days before using.

- Taste. If spice flavor is too strong, add more wine vinegar.

- If bottle is too small to add any additional vinegar, pour some of the steeped vinegar into another clean, dry bottle, making sure to divide spices equally before adding extra vinegar.

Citrus Vinegar

This zesty vinegar is perfect for vinaigrettes, in mayonnaise for a zippy chicken salad, or as a seasoning for seafood. Try it on a mixed salad with fruit, an endive salad with oranges or mandarins, or on celery and orange salad.

Prep time	20 minutes
Cook time	15 minutes
Steep time	2 weeks

Ingredients

- 2 lemons
- 2 limes
- ½ orange
- 1 pinch paprika
- Salt and freshly ground pepper to taste

Preparation

- Zest one of the two lemons, both limes, and the ½ orange.

- In a pot, combine zest with the juice of one lime.

- Add paprika, pepper, salt, and vinegar, stirring well.

- Heat almost to a boil and remove from heat. Do not allow mixture to boil.

- Let cool and pour into a clean, dry bottle. Seal tightly.

- Store in a warm, sunny place for 15 days, shaking bottle occasionally.

- After 15 days, filter vinegar with a sieve covered in cheesecloth and transfer to a clean, dry bottle.

- Seal tightly.

Fresh Herb Vinegar

Delicious in vinaigrettes, mayonnaise-based dressings, or sauces for poached salmon, chicken, smoked pork loin, pasta, avocado, and tomatoes.

Prep time	20 minutes
Steep time	2 weeks minimum

Ingredients

- 2 bundles of one variety of fresh herbs or a combination of roughly chopped fresh herbs (basil, mint, thyme, marjoram, oregano, etc.)
- 4 cups red or white wine vinegar

Preparation

- Wash and thoroughly dry herbs and place in a wide neck bottle.

- Pour vinegar into bottle and seal tightly.

- Store in a dark place to prevent discoloration.

- Let steep for 15 days, shaking bottle daily.

- Taste vinegar after 15 days. If the flavor of the herbs is not strong enough, filter and start again using filtered vinegar and more fresh herbs.

- Store as is or filter again into a new, clean bottle.

Tarragon Vinegar

Use this vinegar flavored with tarragon and dried pink peppercorns to whip up unique salad dressings.

Prep time	20 minutes
Cook time	Simply heat vinegar
Steep time	15 days to 1 month

Ingredients

- 3 branches tarragon
- 3 tbsp dried pink peppercorns, lightly crushed
- 4 cups white wine vinegar

Preparation

- Put tarragon and pink peppercorns into a bottle.
- Pour in hot vinegar.
- Let steep for 15 days or, ideally, 1 month.

Shallot Vinegar

Choose the subtle taste of French shallots for this vinegar, and use in vinaigrettes, sauces, or as a seasoning for oysters.

Prep time	20 minutes
Steep time	15 days to 1 month

Preparation

- Peel and chop shallots..
- Put into a wide neck bottle.
- Pour vinegar into bottle.
- Let steep between 15 days and 1 month.
- Filter and store in a new, clean bottle.

Ingredients

- ½ cup (125 ml) shallots
- 4 cups white wine vinegar

Chili Jalapeño Balsamic Vinegar

Add an intense fiery kick to your favorite meals.

Prep time   20 minutes

Cook time   Simply heat vinegar

Steep time   15 days

Ingredients

- 2 cups (500 ml) balsamic vinegar
- 2 tbsp crushed chilis
- 2 jalapeño peppers, thinly sliced

Preparation

- Bring balsamic vinegar to a low simmer.
- Add crushed chilis and sliced jalapeños.
- Simmer over medium heat for 3 to 5 minutes.
- Remove from heat and let cool.
- Pour into a very clean bottle.
- Store bottle in cupboard and let steep for about 2 weeks.
- Filter and decant into a new, very clean bottle. Store in a cool, dark place.

Old-Fashioned Marigold Vinegar

This extremely fragrant vinegar adds depth to salads, rice, vegetables, and meats.

Prep time	20 minutes
Steep time	10 days minimum

Ingredients

- ½ cup (125 ml) marigold petals
- 4 cups white wine vinegar

Preparation

- Remove spurs and gently wash and dry marigold petals.

- Put petals into a clean, dry wide neck bottle. Add vinegar.

- Seal bottle tightly and place in a bright, sunny place to allow flavors to fully blend.

- Let steep for 10 days or more, shaking bottle occasionally.

- After about 10 days, filter vinegar with a sieve covered in cheesecloth and decant into a clean, dry bottle.

- Seal tightly and store in a cool, dry, dark place.

Old-Fashioned Rose Vinegar

Prep time	20 minutes
Steep time	10 days minimum

Ingredients

- ⅓ cup rose petals
- 4 cups white wine vinegar

Rose petal vinegar has a thousand and one uses, from household to medicinal to cosmetic. For a refreshing facial toner that helps heal blemishes, add 1 part fragrant red rose petals to 8 parts distilled water. It also soothes sunburns and helps reduce acne.

A teaspoon of rose vinegar added to a cup of warm water makes an excellent gargling solution for sore throats and inflammations of the mucous membranes.

Preparation

- Gently remove white petal bases.
- Put petals into a clean, dry wide neck bottle. Add vinegar.
- Seal bottle tightly and place in a bright, sunny place to allow flavors to fully blend.
- Let steep for 10 days or more, shaking bottle occasionally.
- After about 10 days, filter vinegar with a sieve covered in cheesecloth and decant into a clean, dry bottle.
- Seal tightly and store in a cool, dry, dark place.

Variation

- Use ⅓ cup (80 ml) rose petals, tarragon and lavender (2 tbsp each), and 4 cups white wine vinegar, using the same preparation method as the rose vinegar.

Raspberry Vinegar

Delicious with duck, game, and seafood — a pantry must-have for all foodies!

Prep time	20 minutes
Steep time	3 days

Ingredients

- 1 lb fresh raspberries
- 2 ¼ cups (610 ml) white wine vinegar

Preparation

- Reserve 6 raspberries. Put remaining raspberries into a salad bowl and crush to release juices.

- Pour vinegar over raspberries, cover bowl with a cloth, and let infuse for 24 hours at room temperature.

- Filter.

- Put the 6 reserved raspberries into a bottle and pour in vinegar and raspberry mixture.

- Seal tightly and let steep 3 days before using.

Index